HANDBOOK OF PRACTICAL WRITING

Robert A. Butler
Louisburg College

Gregg Division
McGraw-Hill Book Company
New York   St. Louis   Dallas
San Francisco   Auckland   Bogotá
Düsseldorf   Johannesburg   London
Madrid   Mexico   Montreal
New Delhi   Panama   Paris
São Paulo   Singapore   Sydney
Tokyo   Toronto

To Dr. Cecil Wayne Robbins—Louisburg College
president emeritus, Methodist minister, distinguished
journalist, and loving friend

2 3 4 5 6 7 8 9 0 D O D O 7 8 5 4 3 2 1 0 9 8

The editors for this book were Gerald O. Stoner and Alice
V. Manning, the designer was Charles A. Carson, the cover
designer was Ralph Neidich/GAI, the art supervisor was George T.
Resch, and the production supervisors were Kathleen Morrissey
and May Konopka. It was set in Souvenir Light by Trufont.
Printed and bound by R. R. Donnelley & Sons Company.

Library of Congress Cataloging in Publication Data

Butler, Robert Albert, (date)
  Handbook of practical writing.

  Includes index.
  1. English language—Rhetoric. 2. English lan-
guage—Grammar—1950– 3. English language—
Business English. I. Title.
PE1408.B8855   808 '.042   77-27028
ISBN 0-07-009341-5

Contents

Preface

The *Handbook of Practical Writing* is aimed at helping occupational students write effectively and correctly—it addresses both practical writing problems and basic English mechanics.

This twofold function is precisely why I wrote a handbook at a time when hundreds of writing textbooks are published each year. Currently available texts emphasize either the specific occupational demands (such as writing technical reports or reading specification sheets) or the stylistic concerns that are important to the creative writer. While such texts are necessary, there is a need for a handbook specifically designed for the occupationally oriented student who has difficulties in English and who needs basic writing competence.

This book has two distinct parts. The first part includes units that teach the writing of effective sentences, paragraphs, and business letters. Additional units in Part I give hints on how to study, how to sell your skills in the job market, and how to write a term paper.

The second part of the text is a reference to help solve specific problems with mechanics, grammar, and punctuation. Part II is not meant to be a complete grammar of the English language; instead, it is a *selective* grammar which includes only concepts that affect what you put on paper.

A special feature of this book is that it often explains common writing problems in *nongrammatical* terms. Another special feature of the text is that practice tests and answers are provided at appropriate intervals. These practice exercises are designed to help the student prepare for any unit tests the instructor may administer.

The author of a text is always part of a team who work together to create the final product. I am especially indebted to Lynne DeMichele, whose comments provided not only inspiration but also countless improvements in the manuscript; to Gerry Stoner, whose editorial expertise is evident throughout the text; and to Jenny Grissom, my faithful student secretary.

ROBERT A. BUTLER

Part One

UNIT 1

Reviewing Basics:
Learning and Reading Skills

CONTENTS

THE NATURE OF LEARNING

Learning is acquiring new ways of doing things. Learning enables you to perform successfully the tasks necessary for a happy life. Educators agree that an isolated fact that does not help you meet the demands of life is not worth learning. Usually, a fact must be learned in relation to something you are interested in doing. If not, you will have little motivation to retain it.

Learning also involves changes in attitudes, interests, and basic beliefs. Such a change may require developing a completely new behavior pattern, or, it may require strengthening (or weakening) of an old behavior pattern. Scientists and educational psychologists have collected a vast amount of data about the learning process. The list that follows includes those findings which may be of immediate value in improving your study habits:

1. *A combination of whole and part learning is usually recommended.* You should begin by previewing a whole section of material. Then concentrate on the small segments. After you have mastered the small steps, you should go back and connect or relate them to the whole.

2. *It is normal to reach a learning "plateau" when it seems little progress is being made.* During such periods, learning is probably still taking place, but at a slow rate. When you realize you have reached such a period of slow learning, you should either stop to analyze your method of study, or temporarily drop the activity and return to it later.

3. *It is easier to relearn previously learned material which seems to have been forgotten than to absorb new material.* This principle should be reassuring to those of you who are returning to the classroom after a long absence.

4. *Forgetting is caused not so much by disuse as by the interference of new material.* In other words, you forget because new learning interferes with what you already know. You forget more when you study similar subjects than when you study subjects that are vastly different. For instance, trying to study trigonometry immediately after an algebra class would not be as effective as shifting to another subject that is not at all similar to algebra.

Because you tend to remember what you want to remember, you tend to forget things connected with unpleasant experiences. Anxiety, worry, and upsetting emotional experiences can also interfere with remembering important material.

5. *Material you need to retain over a long period of time must be over-learned.* In memorizing the symbols for electronic devices, it is easiest to recall those symbols which you study and repeat over and over again.

6. *A number of short periods of study with a high degree of concentration is far more effective than a long study session.* It is extremely difficult to concentrate on a subject for hours at a time. Your mind will wander, and you will waste much time. Two separate twenty-minute periods of uninterrupted study will yield better results than a whole hour in one sitting.

THE LEARNING ENVIRONMENT

Although your health, motivation, and attitude constitute the heart of the learning environment, the physical setting for learning is also of great importance. The following questions may be used as a checklist to help you study effectively:

1. Is your room well ventilated, and is the temperature between 64 and 68 degrees?

2. Does your desk lamp provide enough light without glare?

3. Is your desk facing a wall that is free of distractions?

4. Does your desk contain only the tools of learning (pencils, paper, eraser, dictionary, and essential books)?

5. Do you work where you will not be distracted by your fellow students?

6. Have you scheduled regular times for study when you will be at your peak efficiency?

CLASSROOM LEARNING

1. *Attend class faithfully.* It is sometimes true that you would learn just as much by sleeping through a class as you would by attending. Nevertheless, students who attend class on a regular basis are more apt to learn more and earn higher grades than students who cut class frequently.

2. *Listen carefully to everything said in class and take notes on important material.* Most instructors have some way of letting you know what is important enough to record in your notes. Some well-organized lecturers write a brief lecture outline on the board. Other instructors will give verbal clues regarding main points:

> "Remember this . . ."
>
> "Most authorities agree that . . ."
>
> "There are four factors which support . . ."
>
> "The evidence suggests that . . ."

Other clues may be repeating a statement, or writing a point on the board. Sometimes an instructor will emphasize a point by speaking slowly, or by speaking in a louder voice. If you watch carefully for the various clues that occur throughout most lectures, you will soon be able to pinpoint the material that should be recorded.

3. *Sit down with another student and compare notes.* This will give you an opportunity to fill in points you missed while the material is still fresh. Putting the material in your own words will go a long way toward fixing it in your memory. Occasionally, it may be necessary to rewrite your lecture notes completely, but that is not a waste of time. The act of writing out the material is another excellent way to learn.

4. *Actively participate in class discussions.* Unless the class is so large that class discussion is impossible, your instructor will appreciate thoughtful and serious questions volunteered by students. Do not wait for your instructor to ask: "Are there any questions?" Think of relevant questions and special points of interest before you go to class so that you will be ready to contribute to any discussion.

HOW TO PREPARE FOR TESTS AND EXAMINATIONS

1. *Study on a regular basis.* Thus, studying for a test will be largely a matter of reviewing the material.

2. *Maintain good health.* Eat properly, get enough sleep, and take time out for recreation and exercise. Pep pills, pots of coffee, and cramming sessions are of little value in studying for examinations.

3. *Write out a summary of your notes* that includes the main points of the material to be mastered.

4. *Talk over the main points and important details* with a friend rather than reread the material.

5. *Pay special attention to the organization of the main ideas* for an essay-type examination. You should be able to recall *in outline form* what you know.

6. *Read all test directions at least twice.* Be certain that you understand what you are expected to do before you answer any questions.

7. *Answer easy questions first* for objective tests. You can then spend the remaining time on the difficult ones.

8. *Pick out key words* such as "compare," "contrast," "prove," or "explain" when taking essay exams and answer the question accordingly. Do not "describe" something if you are told to "explain" it. Give careful attention to handwriting, grammar, and spelling when answering essay questions.

9. *Allow sufficient time to reread your examination,* if possible, and check for careless errors. Do not be tempted to change answers unless you have remembered additional facts.

WHY GOOD WRITING DEPENDS ON YOUR ABILITY TO READ

Why should a book on writing skills include advice about basic reading? You may think that writing is merely written speech—a person who can speak well can write well. On the contrary, good writing must be learned *apart from* spoken language.

A speaker uses body and facial gestures that cannot be transferred to writing. The speaker also changes the tone of voice to give additional meaning to certain words. And a speaker uses simple sentences and short words to achieve clarity.

A writer, on the other hand, cannot use body language or other visual cues, and the audience can review the message early by rereading the passage. Therefore, a writer is not necessarily forced to use short words or simple sentences.

Good writing, then, is not the same as good speaking. To write well you should first *read* the kind of writing you want to imitate and then copy its characteristics in your own writing. The clear *writing* of others provides you with appropriate material to imitate.

HOW TO IMPROVE YOUR READING SKILLS

What happens when your eyes move along lines of print? Special cameras designed to record eye movements have revealed that the eyes sweep across printed lines in quick jerks, with stops in between. Actually, you do not see anything when the eyes jump from one spot to another on a line. Reading takes place only when the eyes stop.

The number of words you see at one glance (or at one stop) is called your recognition span. If you see only one word per stop, your recognition span is very small and you will be a slow reader. People who can take in several words during each stop have large recognition spans and are likely to be good readers.

Another advantage good readers have over poor readers is that they do not pause long at each stop. On the average, your eyes can start and stop again in less than one-fifth of a second, and good readers achieve speed by cutting their stop time to a minimum.

Poor readers tend to retrace their steps by looking back at what they have read. This habit of going backward is called *regression.* It usually occurs because, even though the reader has looked right at the word, the meaning is missed. Since the preceding material was missed, when the reader arrives at the next sentence it may not be fully understood.

From this, you can see that a good reader tries to (1) *increase the recognition span,* and (2) *minimize the stop time.*

1. *Recognition span.* It may be that you are reading one word at a time, and pronouncing each word as you read it. Since ordinary speech may be delivered at a rate of approximately one hundred words per minute, the word-by-word reader is making only about half the speed necessary to become efficient. This habit of moving your lips can be corrected by placing your finger on your lips. Hold them still and try to read faster so that you do not have time to pronounce each word silently.

Another way of improving your reading is to try to pick up a natural grouping of words at each eye stop. In the marked sentence that follows, notice how easy it is to read each phrase or group with one sweep (or stop) of the eye: *On the ninth hole/Betty hit the ball/over the water.* Practice moving your eyes smoothly from phrase to phrase at a sustained rhythm. Reading rhythmically will help you overcome the habit of regression.

One of the best methods of learning to read phrases and natural word groups is to choose several paragraphs of relatively easy reading material, and circle the groups with a pencil. The next step is to practice reading each circled phrase in one eye stop until you have improved your phrase-reading skill.

2. *Minimizing your stop time.* There is no real short cut to minimizing your stop time, except by making a real effort to read quickly. Make a conscious effort to read quickly, but also make sure that you understand what you are reading. Fifteen minutes of regular practice each night will achieve results in two weeks. After your reading speed increases with easy material, you should apply the phrase-reading technique to textbook material.

Remember that you will be able to read storylike material such as history or literature more rapidly than you will read technical data or a laboratory manual. Your goal is to accomplish your various reading purposes at the greatest possible speed.

TEXTBOOK STUDY

1. *Preview the entire text.* Before you begin to study the content of a textbook, you should have a general idea of the material covered by the text. The first place to look is the *preface,* where the author is likely to make a general statement about why the book was written. Second, read the *table of contents.* Third, thumb through the entire book and read the *headings* (usually in **boldface** print). Finally, read any chapter *summaries* that may be included.

2. *Preview each chapter.* A chapter preview is similar to the book preview above. You should read headings and the chapter summary first. Additionally, it is helpful to "skim" through the material by reading the topic sentences that appear in the paragraphs under each heading. Use the headings to determine the author's organization (the outline flow of the chapter). The headings make clear how topics go together and follow each other. They also point out what the main subject of each section is going to be.

3. *Read the chapter carefully and underline main ideas and important details.* A careful reading means that you should read everything, including all graphs and charts. Main ideas are often found in the topic sentence of each paragraph. Details and special terms are sometimes italicized. If a word is not defined within the context of the material, be sure to look it up in a dictionary.

4. *Reread what you have underlined and write out questions and answers on important points.* The act of writing out important material will help you retain it. The process of converting topic sentences and main points into questions you must answer will help you think through the material.

5. *Say the main points aloud, and answer your questions.* The best way to review material is to talk it over with another student who is studying the same subject. Saying the material in your own words will make it much easier to recall. If you cannot find another person to study with, recite aloud to yourself. Do not try to recite too much material at one time. Break up each chapter into convenient sections of material and recite after each section. As review you may then attempt to recite important points from the entire chapter.

6. *Jot down questions about material you do not understand.* As you read through each section, be certain you clearly understand each important concept. If you need help on certain points, prepare a list of questions to ask your instructor or to discuss in class.

INCREASING YOUR VOCABULARY

Vocabulary is another important aspect of reading ability. Good students almost always have a better "working" vocabulary than poor students. Your "working" vocabulary consists of those words you use daily in your own writing and speaking. You also have a "recognition" vocabulary, which is made up of words you recognize in the context of reading matter, but do not actually use yourself.

Although a good vocabulary results from years of listening to intelligent people talk and of reading a wide variety of good books, using vocabulary cards can help build a bigger vocabulary. When you run across a new and useful word, write its definition and a sentence in which it is used on an index card. At convenient times review your new words. Each time you miss a definition, place a dot on the corner of the card and give special attention to those words you tend to miss more than once.

You can also increase your vocabulary if you can figure out what a word means by analyzing its elements. The English language is made up of three kinds of elements: prefixes, suffixes, and roots. Each of these elements has a meaning which is the same in all the words in which it is used. A knowledge of the most common prefixes and suffixes will help you recognize the meaning of many words whose roots are familiar.

A *prefix* is a word part added (fixed) to the beginning of a word. For example, when you read that the President wants to discontinue a particular program, you know immediately that the "dis" part of the word means the opposite or negative of the current situation. The program is currently continuing, and the President wants to cut (or *dis*continue) it.

Recognizing such signals will help you read with increased speed and comprehension. Prefixes which give the most precise clues to words are those that mean *not* or *no*. In the list that follows, each underlined prefix gives the meaning *not* to the word to which it is affixed.

*dis*continued (not continued)
*dis*agree (not in agreement)
*in*consistent (not consistent)
*in*capable (not capable)
*un*happy (not happy)
*un*successful (not successful)
*im*practical (not practical)
*non*commissioned (not commissioned)
*il*legal (not legal)
*ir*replaceable (not replaceable)

The following prefixes are useful because they usually appear in combination with other words.

Prefix	Example	Meaning
anti	*anti*freeze	against
hetero	*hetero*sexual	different
homo	*homo*phonic	same
hyper	*hyper*sensitive	over, in excess
hypo	*hypo*acidity	below, less than
inter	*inter*scholastic	between
intra	*intra*muscular	within
post	*post*war	after—in time
pre	*pre*war	before—in time
pro	*pro*-British	in favor of

Here are some common prefixes and their meanings.

Prefix	Example	Meaning
ab	*ab*sent	away from
bi	*bi*focals	two
de	*de*humanize	away from, down
mis	*mis*take	wrong
trans	*trans*port	across

Suffixes (word parts added to the end of a word) are important clues to word meaning. There are three groups of suffixes: noun, verb, and adjective.

Noun suffixes which mean *act of, state of,* or *quality of:*

Suffix	Example	Meaning
-ancy	occup*ancy*	act of (occupying)
-dom	free*dom*	state of being (free)
-ence	preced*ence*	act of (preceding)
-ency	dec*ency*	state of being (decent)
-ery	brav*ery*	quality of being (brave)
-hood	mother*hood*	state of being (a mother)

-ice	cowardice	quality of being (a coward)
-ion	intercession	act of (interceding)
-ment	argument	act of (arguing)
-ness	fairness	state of being (fair)
-ship	friendship	state of being (friends)

Noun suffixes referring to the *doer* or *one who:*

Suffix	**Example**	**Meaning**
-er	flyer	one who (flies)
-ess (female)	actress	a woman who (acts)
-ist	communist	one who (believes in communism)
-or	debtor	one who (is in debt)

Verb suffixes which mean *to perform the act of:*

Suffix	**Example**	**Meaning**
-ate	perpetuate	to make (perpetual)
-en	shorten	to make (short)
-fy	glorify	to make (glorified)
-ize	terrorize	to make (terrified)

Adjective suffixes:

Suffix	**Example**	**Meaning**
-able	manageable	capable of (management)
-ate	affectionate	having (affection)
-ed	spirited	having (spirit)
-ful	joyful	full of (joy)
-ic	basic	pertaining to (the base)
-ish	bullish	resembling (a bull)
-ive	active	inclined towards (actions)
-less	speechless	without (speech)
-like	childlike	resembling (a child)
-ly	manly	resembling (a man)
-ous	marvelous	full of (marvel)

HOW TO USE THE DICTIONARY

For everyday use a good abridged dictionary is adequate. The following are highly recommended:

Webster's Eighth New Collegiate Dictionary
Funk and Wagnalls Standard College Dictionary
The American College Dictionary

The Random House Dictionary of the English Language
The American Heritage Dictionary of the English Language

The following is a typical dictionary entry, showing you the different types of information you can find there. Different dictionaries may give this information in a different order; if you have any question, there will generally be an explanation in the front of the dictionary.

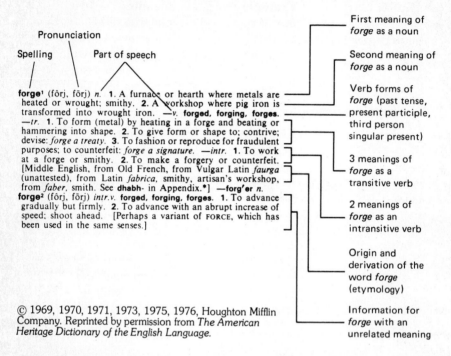

Pronunciation

Spelling   Part of speech

First meaning of *forge* as a noun

Second meaning of *forge* as a noun

Verb forms of *forge* (past tense, present participle, third person singular present)

3 meanings of *forge* as a transitive verb

2 meanings of *forge* as an intransitive verb

Origin and derivation of the word *forge* (etymology)

forge¹ (fôrj, fōrj) *n.* **1.** A furnace or hearth where metals are heated or wrought; smithy. **2.** A workshop where pig iron is transformed into wrought iron. —*v.* **forged, forging, forges.** —*tr.* **1.** To form (metal) by heating in a forge and beating or hammering into shape. **2.** To give form or shape to; contrive; devise: *forge a treaty.* **3.** To fashion or reproduce for fraudulent purposes; to counterfeit: *forge a signature.* —*intr.* **1.** To work at a forge or smithy. **2.** To make a forgery or counterfeit. [Middle English, from Old French, from Vulgar Latin *faurga* (unattested), from Latin *fabrica,* smithy, artisan's workshop, from *faber,* smith. See **dhabh-** in Appendix.*] —**forg'er** *n.*
forge² (fôrj, fōrj) *intr.v.* **forged, forging, forges. 1.** To advance gradually but firmly. **2.** To advance with an abrupt increase of speed; shoot ahead. [Perhaps a variant of FORCE, which has been used in the same senses.]

© 1969, 1970, 1971, 1973, 1975, 1976, Houghton Mifflin Company. Reprinted by permission from *The American Heritage Dictionary of the English Language.*

Information for *forge* with an unrelated meaning

1. *Spelling.* The spelling entry of a word is divided into syllables so that you will know how to separate it correctly at the end of a line. Dictionaries also give the proper spelling of compound words and tell whether a word is capitalized. When different spellings are listed, the first is usually the most common.

2. *Pronunciation.* A dictionary tells you how to pronounce a word by respelling it with a combination of letters and symbols. Keys to the symbols are found at the front of the dictionary as well as at the bottom of the page on which the entry appears. For example, *forge* respelled for correct pronunciation is *forj.* The respelling does not look like English spelling because of the symbols used, but you will know how the word sounds if you consult the key to the pronunciation symbols. A primary accent mark (´) nor-

¹*The American Heritage Dictionary of the English Language,* s.v. "forge."

mally follows the most heavily stressed syllable, and a secondary accent mark (´) follows lightly stressed syllables.

3. *Meaning.* Dictionaries record the past and present meanings attached to words. The Merriam-Webster dictionaries list meanings for the same word in order of historical use, but most other dictionaries list the most general current meaning first. It is best to read all meanings given for an entry before deciding on the best choice.

4. *Etymology.* The origin and derivation of a word help give a complete picture of its meaning. Words tend to change their meaning over long periods of time, and the history of a word is often interesting or humorous.

5. *Synonyms and Antonyms.* Most well-edited dictionaries include a discussion of synonyms (words having a similar meaning) and some dictionaries list antonyms (words of opposite meaning). For a more complete listing of synonyms and antonyms you can refer to a book of synonyms such as *Roget's Thesaurus.*

6. *Grammar.* Dictionaries give the part of speech for each entry. When a word can be used as more than one part of speech, each use is listed along with examples. The principal parts of verbs, the plurals of nouns, and the comparative and superlative degrees of adjectives and adverbs are also listed when such forms are irregular or involve spelling problems.

7. *Labels.* General vocabulary words are not given labels, but words that belong to special fields are given *subject labels* such as medicine, law, economics, and so on. *Usage labels* indicate that a word is restricted in time, geographical range, occurrence, or style. For instance, the label *obsolete* means that a word is no longer used, and *archaic* means that a word has passed out of regular use but may still appear in special situations. Labels such as *dialectal, British,* or *Canadian* indicate that a word is used primarily in certain geographical areas. *Colloquial, informal, slang,* and *substandard* are labels that indicate style. In some dictionaries these subject labels may be abbreviated. If you are not sure what an abbreviation means, look in the list of abbreviations used in the front of your dictionary.

UNIT 2

Building Effective Sentences

As a successful worker, you will need to be able to write complete and well-ordered sentences. This unit serves as a reference guide that will help you eliminate problems in writing the clear sentences your employer will expect in written communication.

A brief index with actual examples is provided so that you and your instructor can locate the material you need to improve your writing style.

CORRECTING SENTENCE PROBLEMS

IMPROVING SENTENCE STYLE

TYPES OF SENTENCES

A sentence is a group of words that contains a subject and a predicate and
expresses a complete thought. A clause is a group of words that contains a
subject and a predicate but that may or may not express a complete thought.

Subject: The word or words naming the person, place, or thing about
which something is said.

Predicate: The word or words telling something about what the subject is
or does.

A brief summary of the four types of sentences is included here to provide a
frame of reference for your study of sentence structure.

1. *Simple sentence.* A simple sentence contains only one clause. The subject or predicate may be compound (a compound subject contains two or more nouns, and a compound predicate contains two or more verbs).

> *Ted handed* the fuse to his assistant. (This simple sentence has one noun, *Ted,* and one verb, *handed.*)

> *Mary* and *John* often *sing* and *dance* at the company party. (This simple sentence has a compound subject consisting of two nouns, *Mary* and *John,* and a compound predicate consisting of two verbs, *sing* and *dance.*)

2. *Compound sentence.* A compound sentence consists of two or more main clauses.

> *Main clause:* A clause which makes a complete statement and may stand alone is a sentence.

> One of the drivers delivered the order of tires, and the other driver picked up a special set of jacks for the truck.

Note: Do not confuse a true compound sentence with a simple sentence having a compound predicate.

> **The construction workers** *were met* **at the bus station and** *driven* **to the site of the new stadium.** (simple sentence with compound predicate)

3. *Complex sentence.* A complex sentence contains one main clause and one or more dependent clauses. A dependent clause is sometimes called a subordinate clause.

> *Dependent clause:* A dependent clause has a subject and a predicate but does not make a complete statement. It shows its dependence by the word which joins it to the main clause.

> You should shut off the main water supply under the house before you call the plumber. ("Before you call the plumber" is a dependent clause.)

Note: Words such as *after, as, because, before, if, since, that, though, unless, until, when, where, which, while, who,* **and** *whom* **are frequently used to introduce dependent clauses.**

4. *Compound-complex sentence.* A compound-complex sentence contains two or more main clauses and one or more dependent clauses.

> Although the fruit growers worked long hours, (dependent clause)

they seemed to enjoy their work, (main clause) and they usually had a long vacation period during the winter months. (main clause)

LEARNING OBJECTIVE
•To eliminate sentence fragments

A sentence fragment occurs whenever a group of words does not express a complete thought. Always remember to complete your thoughts so that sentence fragments do not appear in your writing. A sentence fragment can generally be traced to the omission of a subject or a predicate, or the structuring of the statement as a dependent clause.

After the storm the trees in our back yard. (What happened to the trees? The thought is not complete because there is no predicate. Add the words "were lying" after "trees.")

On the corner near the drug store I saw William. Waiting for the bus to come by. (The phrase "waiting for the bus to come by" is a fragment that should be included in the sentence that precedes it.)

Our trailer is on the south side of the park. At the edge of the woods. (The phrase "at the edge of the woods" should be a part of the preceding sentence.)

The supervisor gave us permission. To go to New York next summer. (The phrase "to go to New York next summer" has been incorrectly separated from the preceding sentence and is therefore a fragment. Simply drop the period and add the fragment to the sentence.)

The clerk wrapped an expensive gift. A gold watch from Germany. (In this example the expression "a gold watch from Germany" is a fragment that has been incorrectly separated from the preceding sentence. Join this expression to the end of the preceding sentence with a comma or a dash.)

We are most grateful for Mr. Anthony's financial assistance. Which made it possible for us to get married. (In this sentence the dependent clause "which made it possible for us to get married" is a fragment which does not express a complete thought. The solution is to use a comma to join this clause to the preceding sentence.)

Note: **Sentence completeness may be tested by locating the subject and the verb, and by determining whether they are introduced by words such as *if, because, since, unless, who, whom, which, that,* and *whoever.* If these words are present, you can be certain that the group of words is a dependent clause rather than a complete sentence.**

Because he left for Denver. (This group of words is a dependent clause.)

Who she is. (The group of words comprising this example is a dependent clause rather than a complete sentence.)

PRACTICE EXERCISE 2-A

In the blank spaces below rewrite the groups of words so that all sentence fragments are eliminated.

1. When the police officer climbed into the patrol car.

_____

_____

2. Adjusting the dials to their correct settings. The lab technician prepared to repeat the carbon analysis experiment.

_____

_____

3. Near the school on the north side of town. Our house trailer is located in the new park.

_____

_____

4. I am thankful for your loan. Which made it possible for me to graduate from the technical institute.

_____

_____

5. We gladly received the new prize. A red and white dune buggy.

_____

_____

6. After the telephone operator gave us the information.

_____

_____

7. On the workbench near the vise. You will find a set of adjustable wrenches.

_____

_____

8. Ms. Lester is in charge of the warehouse. A steel structure built during World War II.

_____

_____

9. Joe asked to see the repair manual. Which was written for students in the new course on auto mechanics.

_____

_____

10. Speaking to the service technicians during their morning break. Mr. Cottrell explained the procedure for connecting the computer analysis terminals.

_____

_____

LEARNING OBJECTIVE

·To eliminate incorrectly joined sentences

1. Sentences are incorrectly joined when two main clauses are carelessly linked together with only a comma between them (comma splice).

> The snow was blinding, the driver could see only ten feet in front of the truck.

2. Sentences are also incorrectly joined when two main clauses are carelessly linked together without any punctuation (fused sentences).

> The snow was blinding the driver could see only ten feet in front of the truck.

You can correct comma splices or fused sentences by one of the following methods:

a. Joining the two main clauses with a semicolon (see pages 188 to 189)

> The snow was blinding; the driver could see only ten feet in front of the truck.

b. Subordinating one of the main clauses (see page 26)

> Because the snow was blinding, the driver could see only ten feet in front of the truck.

c. Joining the main clauses with a comma and a coordinating conjunction (see pages 187 to 188)

The snow was blinding, and the driver could see only ten feet in front of the truck.

    d. Converting each main clause into a separate sentence—

The snow was blinding. The driver could see only ten feet in front of the truck.

PRACTICE EXERCISE 2-B

Correct each of the following sentences in four different ways by using the solutions suggested above.

1. The school play was a huge success, all the children in the first grade were assigned a speaking part.

2. Most of the technical institute graduates who attended the job fair were from our community several of them were able to obtain immediate employment with some of the participating firms.

3. In today's job market, the service industries are an important source of employment, they offer job opportunities to people with various levels of skills, training, and education.

LEARNING OBJECTIVE

•To place the various parts of a sentence correctly

1. Adverbs such as *only, just, even, nearly,* or *merely* should be placed immediately before the words they modify.

She was just asking for a small part. (She was only asking, not demanding.)

She asked for just a small part. (She didn't ask for a large one.)

2. Where a phrase or clause is placed indicates which word or words it modifies. Phrases are usually placed near the word modified or at the beginning or the end of a sentence.

Dad bought a coat for Martha with suede trim. (The coat, not Martha, has suede trim.)

Dad bought Martha a coat with suede trim. (The phrase is placed near the word modified.)

Dr. Daniel described her trip to Africa in our geography class. (The description, not the trip, took place in our geography class.)

In our geography class, Dr. Daniel described her trip to Africa. (The phrase is placed at the beginning of the sentence.)

We bought some golf clubs at a large department store which cost two hundred dollars. (The golf clubs, not the store, cost two hundred dollars.)

At a large department store we bought some golf clubs which cost two hundred dollars.

3. Avoid modifiers that may refer either to a preceding word or to a following word.

We decided on the next day to leave for Europe. (not clear)

We decided to leave for Europe on the next day. *Or,*
On the next day we decided to leave for Europe. (clear)

4. The awkward splitting of infinitives should be avoided; however, those split infinitives which are not awkward are acceptable. (*Note:* An infinitive consists of *to* plus a verb.) As a rule, if the word or words between *to* and the verb can be thought of as part of the verb, the split is acceptable. However, if you have any doubt about this, do not split the infinitive.

To adequately explain the subject within the limits of five pages is impossible. (acceptable)

It offers a view that is to truly be appreciated. (awkward)

PRACTICE EXERCISE 2-C

Correct all misplaced parts by rewriting the following sentences.

1. He was just requesting a three-day pass.

_____

2. Nathan gave a hybrid watermelon to his agriculture instructor with a dark green skin.

_____

_____

3. They sent the oranges to the specialty fruit stores which were grown in California.

_____

_____

4. Susie said during the game Coach Smith acted unwisely.

_____

_____

5. James wanted to, even during his vacation, finish the final chapter of his new book.

_____

_____

6. Your instructor will check the report when you finish for accuracy.

_____

_____

7. The supervisor made some critical remarks about some of the new typists rising from the desk during the evaluation session.

_____

_____

8. Mrs. Martin said during the meeting John acted foolishly.

_____

_____

9. Tell Ms. Adams when she comes to work I want to consult her.

_____

_____

10. It is helpful to immediately pay your bill after the first of the month.

_____

_____

LEARNING OBJECTIVE
·To eliminate dangling modifiers

A phrase or clause that has no word to modify or that appears to modify the wrong word is called a dangling modifier.

> Swimming across the lake, a boat cut in front of Bob. ("Swimming across the lake" is a misplaced modifier because it applies to Bob.)

A boat cut in front of Bob while he was swimming across the lake. (correct)

While listening to the stereo, the telephone rang. (In this example the clause *while listening to the stereo* dangles because its understood subject "we" is not the same as the subject "telephone" in the main clause.)

While (we were) listening to the stereo, we heard the telephone ring. (correct)

To run efficiently, proper maintenance is necessary. (dangling)

To run efficiently, an automobile requires proper maintenance. (correct)

Note: Some phrases are used to modify or introduce the entire sentence rather than to modify a single noun.

Generally speaking, the ice-cream parlor trade decreases during the winter months.

PRACTICE EXERCISE 2-D

Correct dangling modifiers by rewriting the following sentences.

1. When only a small girl, my mother took me to Orlando.

_____

_____

2. Taking our seats, the concert began.

_____

_____

3. To read well, good books must be available.

_____

_____

4. By trimming the hedge once each week, your yard can be beautiful.

_____

_____

5. By rotating the tires at required intervals, that truck should be good for another 10,000 miles.

_____

_____

6. While painting the inside of the garage, the roof was leaking in three different places.

_____

_____

7. Refusing to deliver the order because of cold weather, the manager asked me to accept another assignment.

_____

_____

8. Driving through the city streets at high speeds, several known criminals were spotted by the security officer.

_____

_____

9. To repair my motorcycle, special diagnostic tools are required.

_____

_____

10. Being made of a new type of resilient plastic, I ordered new fenders for my sports car.

_____

_____

LEARNING OBJECTIVE
•To express similar (parallel) ideas in the same grammatical form

1. The basic idea of parallel construction is that you should use the same grammatical form throughout a series of items. For example, if your first item begins with a word that ends in *ing,* then all other items in the series should begin with similar words that end in *ing.*

> Some of the duties of a nurse are *preparing* patients for surgery, *dressing* wounds, and *feeding* those who cannot feed themselves.

Here are some additional examples of parallel constructions.

> Susan's mother decided *to buy a new hat for the reception* and *to have her hair cut.*

Dad promised that he would *take us to the movies* and *buy us some popcorn and candy.*

Chemicals are used *for medicine* and *for cleaning mixtures.*

All our friends are *kind, generous,* and *helpful.*

Rachel spent the day *lying in the sun, reading a novel,* and *drinking soda.*

Note: **The coordinating conjunctions *and, but,* and *or* generally connect similar words and word groups. The correlative conjunctions *either . . . or, neither . . . nor, both . . . and, not only . . . but also,* and *whether . . . or* also connect similar elements.**

2. To make parallel constructions clear, the word that introduces the first part of the construction should be repeated in each parallel element that follows.

(awkward) I admire my friend for his ideals but not his letter-writing habits.

(improved) I admire my friend for his ideals but not for his letter-writing habits. (The preposition *for* is repeated.)

(awkward) She lost a pencil and book.

(improved) She lost a pencil and a book. (The article *a* is repeated.)

(awkward) I feel that he is capable, he will be promoted, and his parents will be proud of him.

(improved) I feel that he is capable, that he will be promoted, and that his parents will be proud of him. (The word *that* is repeated.)

Note: **If it sounds awkward to repeat the word introducing each parallel element, it is permissible to omit repeated words:**

I showed Tony how to set up the projector and how to rewind the film. I showed Tony how to set up the projector and rewind the film. (The repetition of *how to* would be monotonous.)

3. Parallel construction is also needed when the words *than, as,* and *as well as* are used to make comparisons.

(incorrect) *To read* is faster than *writing.*

(correct) *Reading* is faster than *writing.*

Correct each error pertaining to parallelism by rewriting the following sentences:

1. It is easier to teach a seminar on world geography than teaching the entire senior class.

2. To fly is faster than taking the commuter special.

3. Lou photographed an elephant and bird in the state zoo.

4. We heard that the play would be at eight o'clock, the children would be dressed in green suits and dresses, and the parents would be invited to a reception.

5. In our class on auto mechanics we learned to rotate tires, repairing brakes, and to make engine adjustments.

6. Mr. Denton repaired a carburetor and water pump during his spare time.

7. Ms. Jones revealed that the advertising campaign had been successful, business had increased more than thirty per cent, and additional capital was needed.

8. To paint a used car is less trouble than cleaning, polishing, and waxing it.

_____

_____

9. The electrician's assistant explained how to insulate a house for electric heat, how to connect the fuse box to the power source, and conducting safety checks.

_____

_____

_____

10. It is more difficult to repair hydraulic cylinders than replacing brake linings.

_____

_____

LEARNING OBJECTIVE

·_To give variety to your writing style by varying the beginning of sentences_

Some students begin all of their sentences with the subject, and the result is a monotonous style. Study the following methods of giving variety to the beginning of a sentence:

1. In _walked_ your parents.

   (Placing the verb before the subject)

2. White _convertibles_ Jim always admired.

   (Placing the direct object at the beginning; see page 127)

3. _Secure_ he shall never be.

   A captain Henry was at that time.

   (Placing an adjective or a noun from the predicate at the beginning)

4. _Recently_ our team went to Canada.

   Although it did not snow very long, our classes were cancelled.

   (Beginning with a single adverb or an adverb clause)

5. _In the morning_ we shall leave for South America.

On the shelf in the barn you will find the paint brush.

(Beginning with one or more prepositional phrases; see page 176)

6. *To complete the course in arc welding* is his goal.

Walking two miles each morning is an excellent way to improve your circulation.

Soaring along with the help of an ocean breeze, my glider reached a height of ninety feet.

(Beginning with a verbal phrase, like the above; see page 177)

7. *Handsome and talented,* Mr. Rhodes makes an excellent band director.

(Beginning with single-word modifiers)

8. *A constant threat to the environment,* harmful automobile exhaust fumes must be eliminated in the near future.

(Beginning with an appositive; see page 181)

PRACTICE EXERCISE 2-F

Compose ten sentences that begin with some word or grammatical construction other than the subject.

LEARNING OBJECTIVE
•To avoid the choppy style resulting from too many short sentences

Some beginning writers develop the habit of using a series of short, simple sentences. This habit can be corrected by subordination. Observe the subordinating process in the following examples:

Mac Sloan is the manager of a publishing company. He lives on Edgewood Drive in Palo Alto.

Mac Sloan, who lives on Edgewood Drive in Palo Alto, is the manager of a publishing company.

Mac Sloan, the manager of a publishing company, lives on Edgewood Drive in Palo Alto.

PRACTICE EXERCISE 2-G

Create one sentence from each of the following series of short sentences by subordination.

1. Captain Brown is a retired Army officer. He is now employed as a professor of mathematics.

_____

_____

2. Maria Jones teaches Spanish at Northern High School. She lives in the new development near the Lakeview Country Club.

_____

_____

3. Several rolls of wallpaper fell from the top of the ladder. The paperhanger lost his footing.

_____

_____

4. Our crane operator slowly released the cable. The huge ball at the end of the cable crashed against the wall.

_____

_____

_____

5. Ms. Noble is a physical therapist at the veterans' hospital. She lives in an apartment building near the medical complex.

_____

_____

_____

LEARNING OBJECTIVE
•To eliminate the "stringy" style which results from the excessive use of **and** *and* **so**

In ordinary conversation we often tend to string our ideas together by means of the conjunctions *and* and *so*. In writing, however, such a string of ideas is monotonous. In the following examples notice how the stringiness is improved.

Mother said we could have a party in the basement, and I called Juney immediately and told her to bring her record player.

(improved) As soon as Mother said we could have a party in the basement, I called Juney and told her to bring her record player.

(In this example one of the main clauses becomes a dependent clause by subordination.)

She put on her hat and gloves, and then she put on her coat and boots, and then she left our club meeting when the program had finished.

(improved) She put on her hat, gloves, coat, and boots, and left our club meeting when the program had finished.

(In this example, a stringy compound sentence is reduced to a simple sentence with a compound predicate.)

Ray was taking a vacation, and he found it was expensive, so he borrowed money from his uncle.

(improved) When he found that taking a vacation was expensive, Ray borrowed money from his uncle.

(In this example the stringiness is corrected by subordination.)

The game was too long, so we decided to leave during the seventh inning, and on the way home we stopped for hamburgers and Cokes.

(improved) Since the game was too long, we decided to leave during the seventh inning. On the way home we stopped for hamburgers and Cokes.

(In this instance the stringiness is corrected by subordination and division into two sentences.)

PRACTICE EXERCISE 2-H

Rewrite the following sentences to eliminate their "stringy" style.

1. We were in the middle of a boat race and our motor stopped, so Jim quickly discovered that the spark plug was faulty, and he replaced it immediately.

_____

_____

2. Priscilla was working at the dry cleaners, and she soon discovered that the work was hazardous, so she decided to resign and seek another job.

_____

_____

_____

3. He finished waxing the car, and then he painted the garage doors, and then he cleaned out the attic.

_____

_____

4. Uncle Bill said we could play ball in the park, and I told Peggy to bring her glove, and later we started warming up.

_____

_____

5. The electronics instructor was lecturing and he was talking too fast so it was difficult for us to understand his explanations.

_____

_____

_____

LEARNING OBJECTIVE
•To emphasize important ideas by varying the arrangement of the parts of the sentence

In most types of writing, certain sentences may be rearranged to achieve emphasis. Observe how this is accomplished in the following sentences:

1. By placing important words at the end of a sentence

Dr. Smith will gladly accept, in all probability.

(with emphasis) In all probability Dr. Smith will gladly accept.

2. By keeping the reader in suspense and reserving the main idea for the end of the sentence

Practice daily if you want to become a good golfer.

(with more emphasis) If you want to become a good golfer, practice daily.

3. By arranging ideas in such a manner that a logical climax is achieved

The soldiers heard the bombs exploding, the crackling of burning huts, and the popping sound of fiery napalm.

(with more emphasis) The soldiers heard the bombs exploding, the popping sound of fiery napalm, and the crackling of burning huts.

4. By using the strong active voice instead of the weak passive voice

The red wagon was pulled by Tony.

(with emphasis) Tony pulled the red wagon.

5. By repeating important words

This prescription is not valid for narcotics or controlled drugs, and outside the state of California.

(with emphasis) This prescription form is *not valid* for narcotics, *not valid* for controlled drugs, and *not valid* outside of the state of California.

6. By placing words out of their natural order

I really enjoyed this trip.

(with more emphasis) This trip I really enjoyed!

7. By abruptly changing the sentence length

As we drove along the parkway our eyes were straining toward the east in search of a famous skyscraper. At precisely three o'clock in the afternoon the haze cleared away and we saw our objective on the horizon. It was the Empire State Building.

Caution: **By overusing any of the aforementioned devices of achieving emphasis, the writer would create an artificial style.**

PRACTICE EXERCISE 2-I

Write in seven different ways sentences that achieve emphasis.

LEARNING OBJECTIVE
•To write logical, unified sentences

A sentence is logical and unified when all its parts clearly contribute to one idea. The following checklist should help you eliminate elements that hinder the development of logical, unified sentences.

1. Two or more sentences should be used to express ideas which are not closely related.

> (not closely related ideas) The name given the new development near Raleigh, a resort area planned for 10,000 inhabitants, was Lake Sagamore.

> (improved) The name given the new development near Raleigh was Lake Sagamore. It is a resort area planned for 10,000 inhabitants.

2. Avoid excessive subordination.

> (excessive) I recently met a popular singer who looks like a friend who is from the town where I was born.

> (better) I recently met a popular singer who looks like a girl from my hometown.

3. Avoid excessive detail.

> (excessive) Our cabin on Lake Michigan, considered brand new only a few years ago, but now in need of repairs, as is often the case with cabins that are several years old, is being sold next month.

> (better) Our cabin on Lake Michigan, considered brand new a few years ago but now in need of repairs, is being sold next month.

4. Avoid generalizations that lack sufficient evidence.

> (faulty) None of the students in my seminar smoke marijuana. Marijuana is no longer a problem on our campus. (The writer has concluded that marijuana is no longer a problem on the campus merely on the basis of the experience of a handful of students in one seminar.)

5. Eliminate unnecessary words and phrases.

> (excessive words) It was in 1890 that the library was completed.

> (improved) The library was completed in 1890.

> (excessive phrases) In this day and time, it is not easy to locate automobiles that are solid white in color.

> (improved) Locating solid white automobiles nowadays is not easy.

> (excessive words and phrases) As a usual rule the modern colleges of today are large in size.

> (improved) As a rule, modern colleges are large.

6. Avoid the needless repetition of a word or phrase.

> (needless) While swimming in the regional meet, our team of swimmers discovered that swimming early in the morning resulted in the fastest times.

> (improved) While swimming in the regional meet, our team discovered that their fastest times were achieved early in the morning.

LEARNING OBJECTIVE

•*To avoid shifting from one verb tense to another unless there is an actual shift in the time of the action*

1. Tense means time. In English there are six basic tenses (or times) in which action occurs. The present tense (I run) indicates action that is taking place now. The past tense (I ran) indicates action that has already taken place. The future tense (I will run) indicates action that has not yet taken place.

   Somewhat more complicated in their expression of time are the perfect tenses. The word *perfect* in this sense means complete, and the action in the perfect tense has been completed. The present perfect tense indicates action occurring at no definite time in the past (she has worked for us several times) and action occurring in the past and continuing into the present (we have worked here for six weeks). The past perfect tense indicates action that both started and stopped at some definite time in the past (I had completed the project before my last birthday). The future perfect tense indicates action which will be completed in the future before some other future action (she will have seen me again before my plane leaves tomorrow morning).

2. It is important not to confuse the reader by shifting carelessly from one tense to another. The examples that follow illustrate how a tense shift occurs and how the shift can be corrected.

> (careless shift) He made (past tense) a great catch and runs (present tense) down the field for a touchdown.

> (shift avoided) He made (past tense) a great catch and ran (past tense) down the field.

> (careless shift) Mary accepted (past tense) the scholarship and then changes (present tense) her mind.

> (shift avoided) Mary accepted (past tense) the scholarship and then changed (past tense) her mind.

3. It is correct to shift tense when we intend to indicate a change in the time of the action.

(shift correctly achieved) I admire (present) the calmness that Craig showed (past).

(shift correctly achieved) Mr. Baker moved (past) to Denver, where he now manages (present) a ski shop.

PRACTICE EXERCISE 2-J

Correct all errors of tense shift by rewriting the following sentences.

1. She left the class and then had gone to the gym.

_____

_____

2. At twelve noon the secretary reads a statement but refused to answer questions from the press.

_____

_____

3. Jane made some silly remark and rushes down the street.

_____

_____

4. The story is about a woman who achieved great success but loses her health.

_____

_____

5. Jim then invested in the stock market and loses his savings.

_____

_____

ANSWERS TO PRACTICE EXERCISES:

PRACTICE EXERCISE 2-A

1. When the police officer climbed into the patrol car the chase began.
2. Adjusting the dials to their correct settings, the lab technician prepared to repeat the carbon analysis experiment.
3. Our house trailer is located in the new park near the school on the north side of town.

4. I am thankful for your loan, which made it possible for me to graduate from the technical institute.
5. We gladly received the new prize, a red and white dune buggy.
6. After the telephone operator gave us the information, we placed a call to Fairbanks, Alaska.
7. On the workbench near the vise you will find a set of adjustable wrenches.
8. Ms. Lester is in charge of the warehouse, a steel structure built during World War II.
9. Joe asked to see the repair manual(,) which was written for the new course on auto mechanics.
10. Speaking to the mechanics during their morning break, Mr. Cottrell explained the procedure for connecting the computer analysis terminals.

PRACTICE EXERCISE 2-B

1. (a) The school play was a huge success; all the children in the first grade were assigned a speaking part.
   (b) Since all the children in the first grade were assigned a speaking part, the school play was a huge success.
   (c) All the children in the first grade were assigned a speaking part, and the school play was a huge success.
   (d) All the children in the first grade were assigned a speaking part. The school play was a huge success.
2. (a) Although most of the technical institute graduates who attended the job fair were from our community, several of them were able to obtain immediate employment with some of the participating firms.
   (b) Most of the technical institute graduates who attended the job fair were from our community; several of them were able to obtain immediate employment with some of the participating firms.
   (c) Most of the technical institute graduates who attended the job fair were from our community, and several of them were able to obtain immediate employment with some of the participating firms.
   (d) Most of the technical institute graduates who attended the job fair were from our community. Several of them were able to obtain immediate employment with some of the participating firms.
3. (a) In today's job market, the service industries are an important source of employment, and they offer job opportunities to people with various levels of skills, training, and education.
   (b) In today's job market, the service industries are an important source of employment; they offer job opportunities to people with various levels of skills, training, and education.
   (c) In today's job market, the service industries are an important source of employment. They offer job opportunities to people with various levels of skills, training, and education.
   (d) Since they offer job opportunities to people with various levels of skills, training, and education, the service industries are an important source of employment in today's job market.

PRACTICE EXERCISE 2-C

1. He was requesting just a three-day pass.

2. Nathan gave his agriculture instructor a hybrid watermelon with a dark green skin.
3. They sent the oranges which were grown in California to the specialty fruit stores.
4. Susie said Coach Smith acted unwisely during the game.
5. James wanted to finish the final chapter of his new book during his vacation.
6. Your instructor will check your report for accuracy when you finish.
7. Rising from the desk during the evaluation session, the supervisor made some critical remarks about the new typists.
8. During the meeting Mrs. Martin said that John acted foolishly.
9. When she comes to work, tell Ms. Adams I want to consult her.
10. It is helpful to pay your bill immediately after the first of the month.

PRACTICE EXERCISE 2-D

1. When only a small girl, I went with my mother to Orlando. *or* When I was a small girl, my mother took me to Orlando.
2. After we had taken our seats, the concert began.
3. To read well, a child needs to have good books available.
4. By trimming the hedge once each week, you can have a beautiful yard.
5. By rotating the tires at required intervals, Mr. Smith managed to run that truck for another 10,000 miles.
6. While painting the inside of the garage, I noticed that the roof was leaking in three different places.
7. Having refused to deliver the order because of cold weather, I was asked by the manager to accept another assignment.
8. Driving through the city streets at high speeds, the security officer spotted several known criminals.
9. To repair my motorcycle, I discovered that special diagnostic tools would be required.
10. The new fenders which I ordered for my sports car are made of a new type of resilient plastic.

PRACTICE EXERCISE 2-E

1. It is easier to teach a seminar on world geography than to teach the entire senior class.
2. Flying is faster than taking the commuter special.
3. Lou photographed an elephant and a bird in the state zoo.
4. We heard that the play would be at eight o'clock, that the children would be dressed in green suits and dresses, and that the parents would be invited to a reception.
5. In our class on auto mechanics we learned to rotate tires, to repair brakes, and to make engine adjustments.
6. Mr. Denton repaired a carburetor and a water pump during his spare time.
7. Ms. Jones revealed that the advertising campaign had been successful, that business had increased more than thirty per cent, and that additional capital was needed.
8. Painting a used car is less trouble than cleaning, polishing, and waxing it.
9. The electrician's assistant explained how to insulate a house for electric heat, how to connect the fuse box to the power source, and how to conduct safety checks. *or* The electrician's assistant explained how to insulate a house for electric heat, connect the fuse box to the power source, and conduct safety checks.

10. Repairing hydraulic cylinders is more difficult than replacing brake linings.
    or To repair hydraulic cylinders is more difficult than to repair brake linings.

PRACTICE EXERCISE 2-F

Refer to pages 25 to 26.

PRACTICE EXERCISE 2-G

1. Captain Brown, a retired Army officer, is now employed as a professor of mathematics.
2. Maria Jones, who lives in the new development near the Lakeview Country Club, teaches Spanish at Northern High School.
3. When the paperhanger lost his footing, several rolls of wallpaper fell from the top of the ladder.
4. After the crane operator slowly released the cable, the huge ball at the end of the cable crashed against the wall.
5. Ms. Noble, who lives in an apartment building near the medical complex, is a physical therapist at the veterans' hospital.

PRACTICE EXERCISE 2-H

1. Our motor stopped when we were in the middle of a boat race. Jim quickly discovered that the spark plug was faulty and he replaced it immediately.
2. When Priscilla discovered that working at the dry cleaners was hazardous, she decided to resign and seek another job.
3. After he finished waxing the car, he painted the garage doors and cleaned out the attic.
4. After Uncle Bill said we could play ball in the park, I told Peggy to bring her glove. Later we started warming up.
5. Since the electronics instructor was lecturing rapidly, it was difficult for us to understand his explanations.

PRACTICE EXERCISE 2-I

Refer to pages 29 to 30.

PRACTICE EXERCISE 2-J

1. She left the class and then went to the gym.
2. At twelve noon the secretary read a statement but refused to answer questions from the press.
3. Jane made some silly remark and rushed down the street.
4. The story is about a woman who achieved great success but lost her health.
5. Jim then invested in the stock market and lost his savings.

UNIT 3

Paragraphing

CONTENTS

A *paragraph* is a linked series of related sentences that develop one central idea. The central idea of a paragraph is usually stated in a *topic sentence* somewhere in the paragraph. Other sentences list details, provide examples, or offer evidence that support the central idea. Moreover, each sentence should fit into a *logical pattern.* Many paragraphs also have a concluding sentence which summarizes the central idea.

LEARNING OBJECTIVE

•To write a topic sentence

The topic sentence should provide the reader with a complete idea of what a paragraph will say. It must tell what the topic is and what aspect of the topic will be covered in the paragraph.

I work in an auto parts store. I have to do many things, such as wait on customers, stock parts, keep track of the inventory, answer the phone, and give advice on how to fix the various models and types of cars. (This paragraph has a weak topic sentence. It does not say what the topic is and what aspect of the topic will be covered.)

I have to do many different things in my work at an auto parts store. Naturally, I have to keep track of inventory: I make a count of the various parts, stock the new parts being shipped to the store, and get parts from stock for our customers. I also deal with people, both in the store and on the phone. But probably the most demanding task is having to give advice to our customers on how to fix their car, regardless of its age or make.

(I have to do many different things in my work at an auto parts store is the topic sentence. The paragraph is about working in an auto parts store. But more specifically, it alerts the reader to the fact that the paragraph will be about the variety of things that a clerk must do.)

PRACTICE EXERCISE 3-A

Each of the following ideas can be developed in a single paragraph. Think through each idea, and then write a topic sentence you could use to introduce a paragraph on the topic.

1. How to buy a car

_____

_____

_____

2. Description of a citizen's band radio, tape player, or special tool (power saw, electric drill, etc.)

_____

_____

_____

3. Qualities of a good automobile mechanic

_____

_____

_____

LEARNING OBJECTIVE
·*To develop the topic sentence into a paragraph*

Since the purpose of a topic sentence is to state one central idea, usually the topic sentence appears most effectively at or near the beginning of the paragraph. The topic sentence is similar to a learning objective in that it gives the reader a general idea of what is to follow. Although monotony may result if every paragraph begins with a topic sentence, it is best for the beginning writer at least to start with a topic sentence at the beginning of every paragraph.

1. A topic sentence may be developed by facts or details.

> *Breakfast is the most important meal of the day for a serious dieter.* Fruit juice, cereal, bacon and eggs, and toast and coffee will add fewer pounds in the long run than a breakfast of only coffee and doughnuts. Although the larger breakfast contains more calories, it will sustain the dieter through the morning and no snack will be necessary. Additionally, the large breakfast has more usable protein, while the doughnuts have more fattening carbohydrates.

2. A topic sentence may be developed by providing examples. In the following paragraph the writer gives three examples in support of the topic sentence.

> *The extraordinary feats of Ted Williams prove that a great baseball player needs exceptional talents and abilities.* In spite of missing several years of play due to military service, Williams managed to hit over five hundred home runs. Perhaps his most glorious moment occurred when he hit a home run during his last appearance at bat as an active player. Conclusive proof of his talent is also suggested by his overcoming the famous Williams "shift," a defensive strategy that robbed him of numerous base hits. Ted Williams is still remembered as the greatest student of hitting the game has ever seen.

3. A brief story is sometimes used in support of the topic sentence.

> *Serving as a police officer was often dangerous.* On one occasion we received a call to go to a bar that was frequented by young delinquents. As we entered the side door, we could not see the drunken youth standing on top of the bar. Before we could turn around, the youth had jumped on another customer's back and was firing a small pistol into the air. Fortunately, no one was wounded, and we were able to turn the youth over to the county sheriff.

4. A topic sentence may be developed by explaining a point of view or one side of an argument. In a paragraph of this type, the details are used to support the writer's view.

> *You can repair any dent in the body of your automobile, especially dents made by thrown rocks or light collisions with another car.* A professional body repairperson uses special tools, but you can do the job just as neatly and effectively with plastic body filler from an auto-parts outlet. First you have to sand the dented area with 00 sandpaper. Then, use a putty knife to apply a layer of the body filler to

the dent and the surrounding area. When the filler hardens, scrape the area with a Surform grater to shape the patch and remove excess filler. The next step is to sand the area smooth with sandpaper fitted to a block. Do the painting yourself with spray cans of the appropriate primer and color-matched touch-up.

5. A topic sentence may also be developed by definition. In the paragraph that follows, the topic sentence calls for a definition of an alternator.

An automobile's alternator can keep batteries well charged even if the engine is only idling and even while you run accessories (such as the air conditioner, heater, or radio). The alternator is *self-rectifying,* which means that it provides a constant, steady flow of current to the battery with no return flow. This is why a full charge is maintained when the car is idling or operating at a low speed. Of course it is possible to so overload circuits with accessories that even an alternator cannot maintain a full charge with an idling engine, but the ammeter or troublelight on your instrument panel will warn you of overloading.

6. Another method of developing the topic sentence into a paragraph involves comparison or contrast.

The skill of the boxer has often been compared to the grace of the ballet dancer. At first glance, it is obvious that both the boxer and the dancer require rhythm, coordination, a sense of timing, and superbly conditioned bodies. Closer examination reveals also that both must learn to use their feet to achieve certain advantageous positions. What many people fail to realize, however, is that both also need to plan physical movements. Thus, although boxers and ballet dancers may not be friends, they have a great deal in common.

The preceding list of methods of developing topic sentences into effective paragraphs should serve as a general rule for beginning writers. As your skills improve, your instructor will help you discover ways to combine some of the basic methods and to discover additional means of development. No one method, or combination of methods, is better than another except as it happens to suit the needs of a particular paragraph.

PRACTICE EXERCISE 3-B

Use the following or outside references, and your own ideas to develop the following topic sentences into effective paragraphs.

Working Wives[1]

SOURCE: Women's Bureau, U.S. Department of Labor

There were 44.4 million husband-wife families in the United States in March 1970. In 17.5 million of these families—nearly two fifths of the total—the wife was in the paid labor force. In the husband-wife families in which the wife was an earner, the median family income (1969) was $11,629 a year; in those families in which the wife did not work, the median family income was $8,879.

The likelihood of escaping poverty is much greater among husband-wife families when the wife is an earner than when she is not. In 1969 some 2.9 million husband-wife families had incomes of less than $3,000. Only 2 percent of all husband-wife families fell into this income group when the wife was in the paid labor force; 9 percent when she was not.

The higher the annual family income (up to $25,000), the greater is the likelihood that the wife is earning a salary or wages. The labor force participation of wives in March 1970 was lowest (13 percent) in families with 1969 incomes of less than $2,000 and highest (55 percent) in families with incomes ranging between $15,000 and $24,999.

Working Wives and Family Income[1]

A wife thinking about returning to work when her children are relatively grown up should be aware of the oft-repeated saying that two salaries never add as much as hoped to family income. A bigger tax bill and extra expenses for lunches, carfare, clothes, and incidentals take a high toll.

In addition, the amount of money spent on food for the family may rise, for a household with a working wife is likely to eat dinner out more often, or the wife may rush into a food specialty shop on her way home for cold cuts, sandwiches, or frozen main courses, which tend to be more expensive per serving than home-cooked meals.

Moreover, working will frequently prevent a wife from taking advantage of super-market specials or department-store sales. A survey has also revealed that families with working wives often take more expensive vacations than the average family, and they are more apt to have a weekly cleaning woman or other household help, and babysitters.

What, then, are the advantages of a woman's returning to work if she happens to add a relatively small amount to a family's total income?

First: mental stimulation and the feeling that she has at last escaped housework drudgery.

Second: profit, because for most work returnees there must be some financial gain, if only a little, to make the transition worthwhile.

Third: financial security. A woman with a job is working toward higher social security payments than she could perhaps receive as the wife of a retired worker.

---

1. Use facts and details to develop this topic sentence: American women make a significant contribution to the income of their families.

---

[1]New York Times Encyclopedic Almanac, 1972, pp. 495, 498.

_____

_____

_____

_____

_____

_____

_____

2. Use examples to develop this topic sentence: While you may think of a woman as a wife or mother, the fact is that American women are becoming a vital economic force to their families and to the country.

_____

_____

_____

_____

_____

_____

_____

3. Use a story to develop this topic sentence: In the words of a popular advertisement, women "have come a long way" in American society.

_____

_____

_____

_____

_____

_____

_____

4. Develop one side of the argument posed by this topic sentence: Working women are essential to a family's economic status, especially at the lower economic levels.

_____

_____

_____

_____

_____

_____

_____

_____

5. Develop this topic sentence by definition: The problem with economic statistics on "working women" lies in the basic definition of the term.

_____

_____

_____

_____

_____

_____

_____

6. Develop this topic sentence by comparison and contrast: The family is economically better off when both the husband and wife work than when only one works.

_____

_____

_____

_____

_____

_____

_____

LEARNING OBJECTIVE
•Unifying a paragraph

A paragraph has unity when each of its sentences contributes to the central idea of the topic sentence. Any sentence that does not clearly relate to the topic sentence should be omitted.

Caution: **Do not make rambling statements that have a vague relationship to the central idea.**

PRACTICE EXERCISE 3-C

In the paragraph that follows, pick out the sentences that do not contribute to the central idea of the italic topic sentence.

Dad and I have decided to restore a house trailer we built in 1944. Our first task will be to sand and to paint the exterior. The trailer was first licensed in 1946. After the painting process is complete we shall replace the original wiring. The steel bunks we formerly used will be replaced by built-in bunks that will fold away during the day. In one corner we plan to install an ice box, a sink, cabinets, and a counter for a hot plate. In the window over the counter we shall install a fan that will remove excess fumes and cooking odors. The floor will be covered with a new type of linoleum that does not require waxing. Each fall Dad always places a special canvas over the trailer roof to protect it during the winter months. At the front there is a space that we have reserved for a wall-mount air conditioner. The complete restoration should be finished by next summer.

LEARNING OBJECTIVE
•Making a paragraph cohere

A paragraph has coherence when its sentences are logically related to one another. The transition from one sentence to the next should be smooth, and the total effect should show the clear development of the central idea.

1. The first step in achieving paragraph coherence is arranging the sentences in a logical order. Any order which results in a clear thought sequence is satisfactory; however, a number of basic orders may serve as models.

    (a) Chronological (time) order is perhaps the simplest and most common. It is achieved by arranging the details chronologically as in explaining a process—how something is done or made. The following paragraph illustrates chronological order:

        During the last week in February, the land for a new recreational community was offered for sale. By late March, the developers had sold enough lots to pay for their original investment. Many potential customers were requesting lake-front lots, and by June business was so brisk that it was necessary to clear additional land. In September the roads were paved throughout the development and this feature attracted even more buyers. On December 1 the developers announced that all lots had been sold and that the sales office would be closed.

(b) Another basic order of sentence arrangement is the *order of importance.* The least important idea is expressed first, and the others are presented in order of increasing importance. This order is most useful in a paragraph which presents evidence in support of an argument or an opinion.

Employment in electronics manufacturing is expected to increase faster than the average for all industries through the 1980's. The first reason is that large numbers of jobs will open up as experienced workers retire, die, or take jobs in other industries. Secondly, the demand for television sets, stereo systems, video tape recorders, calculators, and C.B. radios will rise as population and personal incomes grow. Finally, government purchases for defense, pollution abatement, and equipment for developing new sources of energy will continue to increase.

(c) Sentences may be arranged to show a *progression* from the general to the particular. In other words, a general statement is made and specific examples or explanations of the statement will follow.

Employees in the paper industry work in a variety of occupations, requiring a broad range of training and skills. Many workers operate and control specialized papermaking, finishing, and converting machines. Some workers install and repair papermaking machinery. The industry also employs many workers in clerical, sales, and administrative occupations.

(d) It is also appropriate to begin a paragraph with a *series of details* and conclude with a *general statement.* When this pattern is used the topic sentence may be the last sentence in the paragraph.

After electricity is generated, it passes through a "switchyard," where the voltage is increased so that the electricity may travel long distances without excessive loss of power. The electricity passes through transmission lines to substations, where the voltage is decreased and passed on to the individual customers. Transmission lines also tie together the generating stations of a single system and the power facilities of several systems. In this way, power can be interchanged among several utility systems to meet varying demands.

PRACTICE EXERCISE 3-D

Each of the paragraphs below lacks coherence. Select one of the methods of achieving paragraph coherence and rewrite each paragraph according to the method you have selected. The answers at the end of this unit will tell you which method is appropriate, but you may need to check with your instructor for an evaluation of your progress.

A. Arranging sentences chronologically (time order)

B. Arranging sentences according to the order of importance

C. Arranging sentences that proceed from the general to the particular

D. Arranging sentences that proceed from a series of details to a general statement

Write the method you select on the first line of the space provided for rewriting each paragraph.

1. Diesel mechanics learn their skills in several different ways. In order to complete their training, many mechanics find it helpful to take courses in diesel equipment maintenance offered by vocational, technical, and correspondence schools. Many begin by repairing gasoline-powered automobiles, trucks, and buses. When employed by firms that use or repair diesel equipment, they receive several months of actual experience in servicing this equipment. Some start as helpers to experienced diesel engine mechanics, becoming skilled in three or four years.

_____

_____

_____

_____

_____

_____

_____

_____

_____

_____

_____

_____

_____

2. When you drive over a bump, for example, and the steering wheel starts to quiver in your hand, it could be a warning sign that a ball joint is going bad. It is important for every driver to become aware of the way in which a worn ball joint will give advance notice of a potentially dangerous condition. Another sign is excessive play in the steering wheel. A third telltale signal that a ball joint needs replacing is a noise from the front that you would normally attribute to the need for greasing.

_____

_____

_____

_____

_____

_____

_____

_____

_____

_____

_____

3. The recent attention given to the shortage of energy in the United States has a rather short history. In the fall of 1973, however, a fuel shortage occurred that quickly became an energy crisis throughout the civilized world. Twenty years ago only a few experts were saying that the earth's natural resources were limited. Nevertheless, most people were not convinced of the seriousness of the energy shortage until the unusually cold winter of 1976-77 caused unemployment, excessively high fuel bills, and a severe depletion of natural gas supplies.

_____

_____

_____

_____

_____

_____

_____

_____

_____

_____

_____

_____

4. In applying the finish coat of an antique kit, you begin by wiping a surface lightly with the cheesecloth wiper that comes with the kit. If, after a few strokes, you are satisfied with the results, you should continue with the same technique. If you are new at antiquing with kits, you will not be long in discovering that the glaze coat is amenable to almost any treatment your imagination can come up with in wiping the top coat. If it is not just what you expected, you should try some other wiper, such as a small sponge, or a brush cleaned in solvent and used dry. Even though several different wipers do not produce the look you desire, you can clean the entire glaze coat off and start all over again.

_____

_____

_____

_____

_____

_____

_____

_____

_____

_____

5. The *orderly arrangement of sentences* is the most basic step in achieving coherence. A second basic step in achieving paragraph coherence is the use of *pronouns* to refer to *antecedents* (words and ideas in preceding sentences).

> Our track coach made a number of strong suggestions to some of the slower runners. *He* asked them to run an extra mile each day after practice to increase *their* endurance. Some of *his* suggestions required the slower members of the squad to eat certain foods and to restrict *their* social life. At the July meeting several of the squad members were asked to turn in *their* uniforms because *they* could not conform to all the new suggestions.

6. A third basic step in achieving paragraph coherence is the repetition of words or ideas in preceding sentences.

> The "southern strategy" has become an important factor in recent elections. In 1968, many southerners who were formerly Democrats voted for Richard Nixon. It has been determined by many experts that the "southern strategy" was the deciding factor in the 1972 election. And by carrying all the principal southern states in 1976, Jimmy Carter managed to defeat Gerald Ford.

7. A fourth basic step in making a paragraph cohere is using transitional expressions.

Caution: **Using such expressions excessively will produce a heavy style.**

> Many colleges and universities are experiencing financial problems. For instance, a recent report has suggested that if current trends continue, certain institutions will be forced to close and many others will begin operating at a loss. For a number of years only private institutions were having financial difficulties; lately, even prestigious state-supported universities are beginning to feel the pinch. Being aware of the financial problems facing our colleges and universities, Congress has now passed a bill which will provide massive federal aid to higher education.

The following guide may be helpful in deciding when and how to use transitional expressions:

To "add on" facts or information, use such expressions as *additionally, also, and, finally, first, furthermore, in addition, moreover, next, secondly,* and *thirdly.*

To express comparison, use *likewise* or *similarly*.

To express contrast, use *at the same time, but, however, nevertheless, on the contrary, on the other hand, otherwise,* and *yet.*

To give the result or the consequence of something, use *accordingly, as a result, consequently, hence, then, therefore,* and *thus.*

To indicate place, use *adjacent to, beyond, nearby,* and *on the opposite side.*

To indicate time, use *immediately, in the meantime, later, meanwhile,* and *soon.*

To summarize, use *in brief, in short, in other words, in sum,* and *to sum up.*

FINAL CHECK LIST FOR WRITING GOOD PARAGRAPHS

1. **Is the central idea either stated in a topic sentence or implied by the paragraph content?**
2. **Is the central idea adequately developed by an appropriate number of details or supporting opinions?**
3. **Is every sentence clearly related to the central idea?**
4. **Is there a smooth flow of thought from one sentence to the next?**
5. **Avoid excessively long paragraphs. As a general rule more than 250 words should not be used in a single paragraph.**

ANSWERS TO PRACTICE EXERCISES

PRACTICE EXERCISE 3-A

1. The first step in buying a car is deciding what your basic transportation needs are.
2. Many citizen's band radios have twenty-three channels.
3. A good automobile mechanic needs common sense as well as the ability to use sophisticated diagnostic tools.

PRACTICE EXERCISE 3-B

Use the methods described on pages 38 to 40 or consult with your instructor.

PRACTICE EXERCISE 3-C

The trailer was first licensed in 1946.

Each fall Dad always places a special canvas over the trailer roof to protect it during the winter months.

PRACTICE EXERCISE 3-D

1. Use method B.
2. Use method C.
3. Use method A.
4. Use method D.

As you rewrite the paragraphs in this exercise, consult with your instructor regarding your use of the various methods of achieving coherence.

UNIT 4

Business Letters and Memos

This unit is designed to provide basic guidelines for practical situations that occur both on the job and in the process of getting a job. Refer to the table of contents below to locate specific material.

CONTENTS

LEARNING OBJECTIVE
•To use correct form in writing business letters

Many employees are faced with the task of writing important business letters. Writing effective business letters is absolutely essential in some positions, and almost any employee who becomes a supervisor will have occasion to write such letters. At top management levels, writing business letters sometimes occupies the major part of the working day.

Business letters should follow standard forms in six necessary parts: (1) heading, (2) inside address, (3) salutation, (4) body of the letter, (5) complimentary close, and (6) signature.

1. The heading should always give the complete address of the writer and the date of the letter.

> 995 North Washington Street
> Kansas City, Kansas 66100
> June 21, 19—

> Fairfax, Vermont 05454
> May 24, 19—

Note: **For a small town such as Fairfax, Vermont, a two-line heading is acceptable.**

If the letter is being written on business stationery that has a printed letterhead, the date may be typed below the letterhead, either beginning at the center of the page or ending even with the right margin. In the full block style (see example, p. 59), the date starts at the left margin.

QUALITY PRINTERS
19 Main Street   Atlanta, Georgia 30304
Telephone 919-803-774

July 2, 19—   or   July 2, 19—

The inverted method of writing dates, which is used by the military services, may also be used in business correspondence. The inverted style proceeds from day to month to year without punctuation.

2 November 19—

2. The inside address is blocked at the left margin and includes the name of the individual or firm and the complete post office address. The name of the state may be spelled out (Wisconsin), abbreviated according to the standard abbreviation (Wis.), or abbreviated according to the two-letter abbreviation approved by the Post Office (WI). The latter abbreviation (WI) should always be used with the ZIP Code. The ZIP Code should be typed two spaces after the state. Do not use a comma between the ZIP Code and the name of the state.

Mr. Randall Alton
209 Tucker Drive
Columbia, SC 29201

In an address, the·name of the state may be spelled out or abbreviated as follows:

	Two-letter Abbreviation	Standard Abbreviation
Alabama	AL	Ala.
Alaska	AK	. . .
Arizona	AZ	Ariz.
Arkansas	AR	Ark.
California	CA	Calif.
Canal Zone	CZ	C.Z.
Colorado	CO	Colo.
Connecticut	CT	Conn.

Delaware	DE	Del.
District of Columbia	DC	D.C.
Florida	FL	Fla.
Georgia	GA	Ga.
Guam	GU	. . .
Hawaii	HI	. . .
Idaho	ID	. . .
Illinois	IL	Ill.
Indiana	IN	Ind.
Iowa	IA	. . .
Kansas	KS	Kans.
Kentucky	KY	Ky.
Louisiana	LA	La.
Maine	ME	. . .
Maryland	MD	Md.
Massachusetts	MA	Mass.
Michigan	MI	Mich.
Minnesota	MN	Minn.
Mississippi	MS	Miss.
Missouri	MO	Mo.
Montana	MT	Mont.
Nebraska	NE	Nebr.
Nevada	NV	Nev.
New Hampshire	NH	N.H.
New Jersey	NJ	N.J.
New Mexico	NM	N. Mex.
New York	NY	N.Y.
North Carolina	NC	N.C.
North Dakota	ND	N. Dak.
Ohio	OH	. . .
Oklahoma	OK	Okla.
Oregon	OR	Oreg.
Pennsylvania	PA	Pa.
Puerto Rico	PR	P.R.
Rhode Island	RI	R.I.
South Carolina	SC	S.C.
South Dakota	SD	S. Dak.
Tennessee	TN	Tenn.
Texas	TX	Tex.
Utah	UT	. . .
Vermont	VT	Vt.
Virgin Islands	VI	V.I.
Virginia	VA	Va.
Washington	WA	Wash.

West Virginia	WV	W. Va.
Wisconsin	WI	Wis.
Wyoming	WY	Wyo.

Longer addresses may include an individual's official position, the name of the firm, and the name of the building.

Ms. Jane Harper, Vice President
Acme Merchandising, The Trade Center
928 North Market Street
Chicago, Illinois 60607

A title should always precede the name of the person. Standard titles include Mr., Mrs., Miss, and Ms. The title Ms. may be used when writing to a woman whose marital status is unknown, and it may be applied to any woman—single or married. Some individuals require special titles, such as Dr. (Doctor), Rev. (The Reverend), Hon. (The Honorable), and Prof. (Professor). *Doctor* is almost always abbreviated as a title, but *Professor, The Honorable,* and *The Reverend* are written in full unless the name is excessively long.

Dr. Robert A. Smith *or* Robert A. Smith, D.D.S.

Professor James Perry *or* Prof. Lawrence Washington

The title should not be confused with the official position. The official position is written in full and follows the name. A comma should separate the name from the official position.

Mrs. Betty Kraft, Director

If the person's name is unusually long the official position may be typed on the second line.

The Reverend Thomas Huntington
Director, Pine View School
1900 Hillcrest Avenue
Asheville, North Carolina 28801

In some instances the official position is of such length that a separate line will be required to type it.

Dr. Clarence Wethington
Superintendent of Schools
847 Main Street
Portland, Oregon 97208

Street names represented by the numerals *one* through *ten* are spelled out. From *eleven* on, figures are used with or without ordinal endings (st, as in 1st; nd or d as in 2nd or 2d; etc.).

209 Eighth Street

223 North 12th Street

804 East 13 Street

When the street name is a number above ten without a direction following the house number, always use the ordinal ending. You may also use a *space hyphen space* to separate the two items.

904 20th Street

904 - 20th Street

When a building number is represented by the digit 1 (one), spell out *One*. Use figures for all other building numbers, including the other single digits.

One Highland Drive

9 Highland Drive

North, East, South, and *West* and their combinations are not abbreviated when included as a part of street addresses.

Miss Karen Stevenson
325 North Blount Street
Lago, Texas 79910

Sectional divisions of cities are abbreviated and follow street names.

917 Edgewood Drive, N.W. (*or* NW)

Remember that the inside address is always identical to the address that appears on the envelope.

3. The salutation (or greeting) is written flush with the left margin two spaces below the inside address and is followed by a colon. The first word and all nouns in the salutation are capitalized.

Gentlemen: (for a firm composed entirely of men)

Ladies: or Mesdames: (for a firm composed entirely of women)

Dear Mr. Bolton: (personalized salutation for a man)

Dear Mrs. (Ms.) (Miss) Crump: (personalized salutation for a woman) Always use the title a woman prefers if you know it. If you do not know, use Ms.

Dear Sir or Madam: (to address an individual whose name the writer does not know)

In some cases a business letter is addressed to an organization but marked for the attention of a particular individual. In such letters, the "attention line" is typed two lines below the inside address and two lines above the salutation. The usual placement for the attention line is flush with the left margin. No punctuation is needed following the word "Attention," although a colon is sometimes used.

Attention Ms. Barbara Jackson

or

Attention: Mr. Harry Pittman

or

Attention Department Manager

4. The body of a typewritten business letter is single-spaced, with double spacing between paragraphs. All paragraphs should either begin flush with the left margin or be indented five spaces.

Long paragraphs are not desirable in business letters. Each paragraph should represent a unit of related thought that is expressed as clearly and as briefly as possible. Variety in paragraph length increases the appeal of business letters. A short opening and a short closing paragraph help give balance to paragraph length. Always avoid writing only one line of a new paragraph at the top or at the bottom of a page.

When a letter requires a second sheet, use plain stationery of the same color and quality as the sheet that bears the letterhead. As a rule the second and succeeding sheets do not carry a printed heading. Plan the length of a two-page letter so that at least two or more lines are carried over to the second page. It would be awkward to use the second sheet for the complimentary close and signature alone. On the second page and succeeding pages it is necessary to type a heading which consists of the first line of the inside address, the date, and the page number. This heading should begin one inch from the top of the sheet.

Mrs. Bess Wilson—2   July 1, 19—

or

Mrs. Bess Wilson
Page 2
July 1, 19—

or

Mrs. Bess Wilson   2   July 1, 19—

5. The complimentary close is determined by the tone and degree of formality expressed by the salutation. Ordinary business letters addressed to strangers should close with *Yours truly,* or *Very truly yours.* When a business letter is addressed to an individual with such an opening as *Dear Ms.*

Black, the more friendly *Yours sincerely, Sincerely yours, Cordially yours,* or *Sincerely* may be used. Capitalize only the first letter of the complimentary close, and put a comma after the last word. Double-space between the main body of the letter and the complimentary close.

6. Type the name and the official position of the writer four spaces below the complimentary close. If the official position is very long it may be typed on the line beneath the name.

> Sincerely yours,
>
> *Jackson B. Coleman*
>
> Jackson B. Coleman
> Superintendent of County Schools

The name is handwritten in the four spaces that separate the complimentary close from the typed name. The name should be handwritten exactly the same way that it is typed.

Neither professional titles nor degrees should be used with the handwritten signature, but a woman may indicate her preferred title in parentheses. Also, a man should include Mr. in parentheses if his name is one that can belong to a person of either sex.

> (Miss) *or* (Mrs.) *or* (Ms.) Mary Ellen Smith
>
> (Mr.) Beverly Smith

The identifying initials of the dictator and the transcriber (typist) are usually placed two spaces below the last line of the typed signature and flush with the left margin. The dictator's initials usually precede the initials of the transcriber. In the examples below *ASB* dictated and *gh* typed.

> ASB:gh   or   ASB:GH

In some business offices numbers are assigned to the stenographers to be used in place of identifying initials.

> RNP-12

When a business letter refers to an enclosure, the stenographer should make a notation of the enclosure by writing *Enclosure* or *Enc.* two spaces below the identifying initials.

> Enclosure: Personal Data Sheet

When copies of a business letter are mailed to more than one person, a reference to each recipient should be specially noted two spaces below the identifying initials.

> cc: Mr. Taylor   or   Copy to Mr. Taylor

August 19, 19--

Mr. Walter R. Bryant
State Trucking Company
2010 Martin Avenue
Albany, Georgia 34602

Dear Mr. Bryant:

We can supply you regularly with tractor-trailer repair service and guarantee
our work for sixty days. Our company maintains four major motor pools; the
southeast pool, which is located just outside Atlanta, would serve you.

Our rates are based on union wages and have been acceptable to the great majority
of our customers. All our mechanics are required to undergo a thorough evaluation of their competence every six months.

I shall be in the Albany area next month to explain the details of our proposed
contract. We are looking forward to serving you.

Sincerely yours,

JRSwanson

James R. Swanson
Service Representative

JRS:mk

Characteristics: **The extreme (or full block) style is easy to type because
each line begins at the left margin. This style is considered to be vigorous
and aggressive.**

854 Spring Street
Gary, Indiana 46401
August 19, 19--

Mr. Robert Stevens, President
Central Motor Company
407 South 68th Street
Chicago, Illinois 60607

Dear Mr. Stevens:

Mr. Charles Stanley, your representative at the recent Job Fair, suggested that I write to you regarding the opening in your service department.

On the enclosed personal data sheet I have listed my education and work experience that would qualify me for the position of assistant service manager in your organization. My most recent employment as a technician in the engine assembly division has helped me to decide to pursue a service position as my permanent career.

I shall be glad to come to Chicago for an interview at any time that is convenient for you. Please call me at (312) 885-7789.

Very truly yours,

Malcolm Adams

Enclosure: Résumé

Characteristics: The modified block style is used more often than any other letter style. The paragraphs usually begin at the left margin, but they may also be indented. The heading and complimentary close are lined up with the center of the page.

LEARNING OBJECTIVE

·To divide words correctly at the right side margin of business letters, memos, and reports

In business letters, reports, and term papers, the division of words at the end of a line should be based on principles of spelling, pronunciation, and balance. In this instance balance means retaining a readable portion of the divided word on the first line. In other words, it is preferable to have enough of the word appear on the first line to suggest the entire word and to carry over to the next line enough of the word to have two reasonably sized parts.

Words should be divided only between syllables. One-syllable words such as *strength, thought* or *through,* should never be divided.

More than one letter should be included with the part of the word on the first line and more than two letters with the part carried over to the next line.

teacher *not* teach-er   around *not* a-round

Always try to avoid dividing a word of six or fewer letters even though it may have two syllables.

letter *not* let-ter   sudden *not* sud-den

When a root word ends in a double consonant before a suffix is added, divide between the root word and the suffix.

spell-ing *not* spel-ling

Endings such as *cial, cion, sion, sive, tial, tion,* and *tive* should be retained as separate units.

Do not divide figures, abbreviations, and contractions

$20,000 *not* $20,-000   A&P *not* A&-P

couldn't *not* could-n't

If possible, avoid dividing the last word of a paragraph or the last word on a page.

If it is necessary to divide parts of a proper name, a date, or an address, divide at logical points that will make the whole item easy to read.

John D. - Smith *not* John - D. Smith

June 15, - 1980 *not* June - 15, 1980

Newark, - New Jersey *not* Newark, New-Jersey

When in doubt, consult a dictionary or a special word division manual.

LEARNING OBJECTIVE

·To examine the appropriate format for memos

A memorandum is essentially a written reminder to carry out a specific task. Most firms use printed memorandum forms for brief, informal messages.

Short messages that require a rapid response are usually handwritten. The top of a printed memorandum form provides space for headings covering *to*, *date*, *from*, and *subject*, as in the following example:

```
To:       Ms. Jan Smith              From:  Mr. Steven Anderson

Subject:  Request for one additional  Date:  October 20, 19--
          typist and one electric
          typewriter in the editorial
          department


          Because of the increased amount of work in the editorial department, I request
          one additional typist and one electric typewriter.  This request is based on
          the following data obtained from payroll records and the Central Machine Company
          sales representative:

          1.  During the past six months, the demand for typing output has increased.
              This extra work has cost the company $62.00 per day in overtime expenses.

          2.  At current rates the salary of one additional typist would be $42.00 a day.

          3.  The cost of the additional electric typewriter would be approximately $675.00.

          4.  Therefore, our saving in overtime expenses of $20.00 a day would pay for the
              new equipment in 33 and 3/4 days.
```

LEARNING OBJECTIVE

·To examine the appropriate format for informal reports

A longer memorandum used to communicate the results of an investigation is an informal report. The format for informal reports is as follows:

Date	Date
To	To
From	From
Subject	Subject
Introduction	Introduction
Purpose	Purpose
Problem	Conclusions
Scope	Recommendations
Body	Problem
Presentation and	Scope
interpretation of data	Apparatus
Conclusions	Procedure
Recommendations	Body
	Presentation and
	interpretation of data

Note: **In both the preceding report outlines, the scope of the report does not have to be stated separately if the statement of the problem defines it.**

UNIT 5

Getting a Job

INTRODUCTION

In the course of your recent training, you have developed a highly marketable commodity—your own occupational skills. These skills are potentially valuable in the job market. However, as any marketing expert will tell you, a product must be more than salable: it must be *sold* before its potential value can be realized.

In the job market, you are the "product"; the prospective employer is the "buyer." This unit proposes to guide you in the selling process necessary to gain the best position available for you.

First, you must look at the current job market in your field to know where you stand as a candidate. Next you should determine the various ways to discover specific job openings. Then you must make a realistic appraisal of your personal and vocational assets and try to determine how best to present yourself to the market you have discovered. Finally, you begin the process of applying for a specific job or jobs, including preparing a résumé and planning for an interview.

WHERE TO LOOK FOR A JOB

Before you begin job hunting, you should determine where you would like to work. You may wish to establish yourself in the city, or perhaps you would prefer to live in the country. Would you be happier in a small-town atmosphere than in a large metropolitan area? To a large extent, the kind of job you seek may limit your options.

A few large employment agencies advertising in periodicals such as the *Wall*

Street Journal are prepared to place people in almost any given area. If you have a specific region in mind, you can write to the Chamber of Commerce or local state employment office requesting information about a particular market or even a recent copy of local classified ads. This should give you some company names to which you can send a letter and résumé. Also, do not overlook as sources of information any acquaintances or relatives living in the desired area.

Job research in your own area is somewhat easier because information is more accessible. You should begin using some of the following approaches to your job market research weeks in advance of the date you will be available for the new job.

INSTRUCTORS, ASSOCIATES, ACQUAINTANCES IN THE FIELD

Your instructors are in touch with people in your field and keep abreast of changes in your area of the local job market. If you are looking for a particular kind of job or location, make sure your instructors are aware of the fact.

Exchanging information with classmates may also be helpful. A position unsuited for one may be quite appropriate for another. In addition, you should contact anyone you know who works in the field for suggestions of potential employers or for notices of upcoming job vacancies.

PRIVATE EMPLOYMENT AGENCIES

Employment agencies are in the business of matching jobs to people. Many of them specialize in a particular work area; there are even overseas agencies which specialize in placement in foreign countries. If you look carefully, you may find one which seems to fit your particular needs. Usually, in each city a few select personnel agencies are affiliated with the Inter-City Personnel Association. This is a kind of national multiple listing system which enables affiliates to place people in any area of the country.

Any of these employment services will require that you fill out an application and/or submit a résumé. Many of them are informed of job openings not publicly advertised and can give you a number of appropriate leads to investigate. In some cases you will have to pay the agency a fee for this service, which you pay when a particular position is found for you. The amount is usually determined by the kind of job you seek.

Some positions are designated "fee paid." This means the company will underwrite the cost of the agency service. You may be reimbursed for all or part of the fee by the company after a given period of time. Regardless, make sure you read thoroughly any contract you sign with an agency so that you know exactly what your obligations will be.

Agencies can save you some time by screening out all but the jobs most suited to your qualifications. However, it is best not to depend on an agency entirely. Your best interests will be served by using a combination of job-hunting methods.

STATE EMPLOYMENT SERVICE

The local office of the state employment service (or employment security division) is a good source of information on the job market in your particular area. This state service provides testing, counseling, and placement in a complete range of occupations from unskilled to professional. The clearance officer there can inform you of job listings in other parts of the state.

The testing service provided can be useful in determining your aptitude for a particular kind of work and your individual preferences. As a student completing a period of training in a given field, you may find it helpful to take the preference test administered by the service. This will help you get an idea of which of the special areas to which you might apply your education will give you the greatest degree of personal satisfaction.

Those who are handicapped, who have police records, or who have other special difficulties hampering their marketability will find at the state employment office special help which may not be available elsewhere. Many local business associations and industries cooperate with the state office in providing positions for such people.

If you are a *veteran,* you should make it a point to contact your representative at the local state employment service. You can receive additional services and special consideration in applying for a job.

In summary, there are several advantages to using the services of the state employment office over those of a private concern: greater diversity of job listings, individualized testing and counseling, and no fee to pay.

CIVIL SERVICE

Your area Civil Service Commission office tests, interviews and hires personnel for a wide variety of government jobs in such areas as offices, laboratories, hospitals, machine shops, national parks, electronics, meteorology, or research. People are placed throughout the United States and in some foreign countries.

Most types of jobs found in business and private industry are found in Civil Service. However, each area office accepts applications for only those positions which need to be filled.

Information provided by your local office includes:

Federal employment opportunities outlook

Vacancies in shortage categories—occupations in high demand

Job requirements and qualifications

Applications and examination procedures

Special employment counseling services

These centers are specially equipped to provide you with a full range of federal employment information. The information specialist who answers your inquiry can send you such current printed materials as:

Job announcements

Application forms

Pamphlets describing special employment programs

The job announcement will specifically explain job duties and responsibilities and the required qualifications. Read these carefully before applying; if you do not meet given specifications, you cannot be considered. You may, however, receive credit for unpaid experience or volunteer work if you feel it represents "qualifying experience" for the position you seek.

When you apply at a Civil Service office for a position, you will be examined by a written test, performance test, and/or interview. Then if your work experience, training, and aptitude meet job requirements, your name, along with those of the other qualified applicants, will be forwarded to the federal agency seeking new employees. The final decision to hire is then made by the agency itself usually after another interview.

There are some advantages to considering applying your training in the Civil Service. Benefits are excellent, you do not pay social security (Civil Service has its own retirement fund), veterans and the disabled receive special consideration, and job security tends to be greater than in private industry.

NEWSPAPER ADS

Regardless of what other methods you choose to use in looking for work, you should get into the habit of regularly studying the help wanted sections of all the area newspapers. People and companies seeking to hire, as well as employment agencies, advertise in these sections. You may find either an agency to contact which specializes in your general work area, or a number of specific positions for which you qualify.

Daily reading of the classifieds is important because new job openings appear constantly. If you find one that interests you, call or send a résumé immediately, as there are frequently many applicants, and a position can be filled quickly.

BLIND ADS

Often ads appear which give no employer name—only a blind post office box number or phone number. Be cautious of these because there are a number of possible motives behind them, many not in your best interests.

Occasionally, when a small business or a professional individual advertises a job opening, it is simply less disruptive of office activities to have applicants send résumés to a blind box number so they may be screened at a convenient time and only the best prospects contacted. This cuts out numerous incoming calls and callers.

However, some other common reasons for using an anonymous ad are perhaps less honest:

1. The ad may be only a device for obtaining data on a geographical job market, possibly for an industrial concern which is considering establishing an operation in the area.

2. Some companies conceal their identity in an attempt to quietly "steal" employees away from a competitor. This usually happens in cases where some prior commitment contrary to such a practice has been made.

3. Occasionally the blind ad may be a ploy to determine whether or not any employees are dissatisfied. The ad is placed with the idea of discovering if any of the company's own employees apply. It is also an effective technique for securing information regarding salaries paid by other employers.

Other less common reasons for using a blind ad arise from a specific need for privacy, but as a job hunter you should be wary of them.

TRADE PUBLICATIONS

Every technical field is represented by a trade journal, newsletter, or some other kind of publication. Check to see which ones are available at your local branch library. Such publications usually devote a section to job openings— usually for more advanced, upper level positions. However, this kind of research should help you get a perspective on the range of your job market, upper-level pay expectations, and specializations in demand.

BULLETIN BOARDS

Many of the larger concerns employing people in your field will post descriptions of in-house job openings on bulletin boards in the personnel department and other places where employees congregate.

If you work in such a place, make it a point to check regularly for these notices. Often it is to your advantage to apply for such positions, as some companies make a practice of trying to hire from within before advertising a position publicly. You might also ask friends or relatives to check for job openings where they work. This is one way of hearing of a position in your field before it appears in the classified ads, or of some positions which would not be advertised at all.

THE APPLICATION FORM

Practically all places of employment require you to fill out an application form. The format will vary from place to place, but certain information is basic to all. Before applying for a position you should have collected all your personal data including education, job record, references, and all pertinent dates. (See sample application, p. 69.) If you can get an application form from the company before your interview date, you can type it. This is more convenient for you and usually looks better to the prospective employer.

For best results in completing an application form, follow these steps:

1. Read and follow all directions exactly.

2. Read each question carefully before answering.

3. Print or type neatly unless otherwise directed.

4. Avoid leaving blanks. If your answer to a question is negative write "no" or "none." If the question is not applicable, write "N/A."

5. Make sure you have dated the form correctly and have signed your name.

6. Secure permission ahead of time from those whose names you wish to use as references. Use the following as a guideline unless otherwise directed:

> One instructor who can attest to your technical competence
>
> One work reference—someone who is familiar with your attitude and sense of responsibility as an employee
>
> One character reference—someone who is respected in the community who has known you for a long period

If the application calls for "personal references" you should assume that names requested are people *other* than those for whom you have worked.

Note: **You are not bound to answer any questions regarding race, religion, politics, age, or disability not affecting your work competence.**

Stonecrest

120 Main Street
Frenchtown, N.J. 08825

311 936 6640

The Law Prohibits Discrimination Because of Age, Sex, Religion, Race, Color, and National Origin and Requires Affirmative Action in the Hiring of the Handicapped and Veterans.

Personal Data

Please Print in Dark Ink or Type

Name _____
Last   First   Middle Initial

Present Address _____
Street

City _____
State   Zip Code   State   Zip Code

Telephone   Area Code   Number

Permanent Address*
Street

City _____

Telephone   Area Code   Number

* Leave blank if same as present address

Please check if you are   US Veteran ☐ No   ☐ Yes (Indicate Date of Separation _____

☐ 18 or under (indicate age _____)   ☐ 65 or over

US Citizen   ☐ Yes   ☐ No   If No, indicate Type of Visa _____
                                          and
                                          Alien Registration No. _____

Have you ever   ☐ been employed by   ☐ previously applied to Stonecrest?

Employment Experience

Please list your job history for the past ten years (or last four employers). Start with your present status and note any periods in which you were not employed.

Include U.S. military service (show rank/rate at discharge *but not* type of discharge), previous Stonecrest experience, summer/part-time jobs, and cooperative education assignments.

Company Name and Address	Dates Employed		Base Rate of Pay	Position Title and Description of Duties	Reason for Leaving
	Month	Year			
Name _____	From ___	___	Starting ___ Per ___	_____	_____
Address _____	To ___	___	$ ___ Final Per ___	_____	_____
Name _____	From ___	___	Starting ___ Per ___	_____	_____
Address _____	To ___	___	$ ___ Final Per ___	_____	_____
Name _____	From ___	___	Starting ___ Per ___	_____	_____
Address _____	To ___	___	$ ___ Final Per ___	_____	_____
Name _____	From ___	___	Starting ___ Per ___	_____	_____
Address _____	To ___	___	$ ___ Final Per ___	_____	_____

Do you have any objections to our contacting your present employer to verify the above?

□ No, you may contact anytime.   Area Code ___   Number ___   □ Do not contact now; you may contact at a later date. (Please specify: eg, after acceptance of offer or a specific date if appropriate) _____

Your Job Requirements

Type of Work Desired

Work Location Desired

Salary Desired $ _____ Per _____

If you were asked to consider employment at another Stonecrest location, do you have a geographic preference?

☐ Yes   ☐ No   ☐ Would not consider another location

If Yes, please specify.   1. _____

2. _____

The following conditions may be required at some point in a job assignment. If required, would you be willing to work:

a. Shift Work?   ☐ Yes   ☐ No

b. Overtime Work?   ☐ Yes   ☐ No

c. Rotational Work Schedule?   ☐ Yes   ☐ No

d. Work Schedule Other than Monday through Friday?   ☐ Yes   ☐ No

When could you be available to begin work?

Check appropriate box for type of employment

☐ Regular   ☐ Part-Time   ☐ Temporary   ☐ Summer   ☐ Cooperative Education

Education and Training   *Please complete all appropriate items.*

Type of School	Name and Address of School	Dates Attended From Mo/Yr	To Mo/Yr	Graduated Yes	No	Type of Degree, Diploma or Certificate and Major/Minor Fields of Study	Academic Standing Grade Average out of Base (eg 3.2/4.0)	Class Quartile
High School (Last Attended)								
All Vocational Schools, Technical Institutes and Junior Colleges								
All Colleges or Universities								
Other Training Include Military Schools and Equivalency Diplomas								

Academic Achievements and Activities:
Please list academic honors, scholarships, or fellowships; memberships in academic honorary societies; or participation in or offices held in extra-curricular activities you consider significant.

(You may exclude all information indicative of age, sex, race, religion, color, national origin, and handicap.)

List machines you can operate, licenses, certificates of ability, special training, etc. _____

The information that I have provided on this application is accurate to the best of my knowledge and subject to validation by Stonecrest.

Signature of Applicant _____   Date _____

YOUR RÉSUMÉ

WHAT IT IS

A "résumé" is sometimes called a "data sheet," "profile," or "curriculum vitae." In any case, it is a kind of personal summary which represents you to a prospective employer. It is an efficient way of convincing an employer to interview you. Then, after the interview, it can serve as a reminder and as a means of distinguishing you from among a number of other applicants.

The résumé is important in addition to an application because it is made to fit your background and abilities. It can emphasize certain aspects and provide significant detail for which a company application form is not designed. Therefore, you should prepare it as carefully as an advertising copy writer prepares sales copy.

Before you begin drafting your résumé, you should be aware of the available résumé styles and formats. The three most common formats are *chronological, functional,* and a *combination of the two.* If none of these suits your needs, there is another possibility called the *résumé alternative.* You should choose the format that best presents the points you wish to emphasize to a prospective employer—and plays down any negative information.

1. The *chronological* résumé is the most widely accepted format and the one with which employers are most familiar. It is also the easiest to write. Jobs are listed in chronological order, starting with the most recent (which generally receives the greatest emphasis) and working back through the years. Employment dates are listed first, followed by the name of the company, and then the job title. The chronological résumé stresses a steady employment record (without much job hopping). Its main disadvantage is that employment gaps and/or lack of job experience are starkly revealed.

2. The *functional* résumé does not list specific jobs or specific dates. It is organized instead to highlight the qualifications of the applicant. It stresses selected skill areas that are marketable and in demand. Instead of giving equal weight to each job held, it lets the job applicant emphasize or play down past job duties.

3. The *combination* format is just that: it emphasizes job skills (functional) and includes specific company names and dates (chronological) in a separate section. The combination format allows an applicant to stress the most relevant skill areas, and at the same time satisfies the employer's desire for specifics.

4. The *résumé alternative* is a special letter written to a particular person in a company about a specific job. It takes the place of a résumé in certain cases. If, for example, you are looking for a job in a field in which you have no related experience, this option may be your best bet. The purpose of

```
                                        1722 Mape Drive
                                        Sonoma, CA  92318
                                        (213) 787-2596


        Mr. Jerome P. Edelman, Shorthand Supervisor
        Gregg Division
        McGraw-Hill, Inc.
        1221 Avenue of the Americas
        New York, NY  10020

        Dear Mr. Edelman:

        Dr. Paul Parish at the USC Graduate School suggested that I contact you about
        the new shorthand terms workbook that your firm is currently planning.  He also
        mentioned that you might be thinking of hiring someone to coordinate the sec-
        tion on data processing.

        As a working secretary with a shorthand speed of 80 wam, I have had experience
        with the Gregg shorthand system.  I have also been taking courses in computers
        and working on the data-processing system at my company.  I am certain that my
        familiarity with shorthand and with the operations of the computer would enable
        me to facilitate your research on finding data-processing terms to convert to
        shorthand symbols.

        In addition, I have read widely on my own about the office systems of the future
        and could incorporate some of that knowledge into a separate section of the
        data-processing chapter of the workbook.

        I plan to be in New York next week and wonder if we could get together on
        Wednesday or Thursday for an interview.  I'll call you to confirm when you
        will be available.

                                        Yours truly,



                                        Diane Sime
```

the letter is to emphasize your skills and accomplishments and to show how they would lend themselves to an employer's specific needs. This requires some research on your part into the company's business prospects. (Research can be a simple matter of reading company brochures, annual reports, and advertisements. You can also consult Standard & Poor's Register, Dun & Bradstreet directories, and the Standard Directory of Advertisers for more information on the company as well as the name of the person who heads the division in which you are interested in working.)

Remember, though, that the résumé alternative can only get you an interview. Once you have an appointment with your contact, you would be well advised to have a real résumé with you as a capsule description of your accomplishments.

FORMAT

The following is a basic outline to follow in organizing the information on your résumé. This is only a guideline. You may wish to rearrange information or delete sections which do not apply:

Name
Home Address
Phone Number

Job Objective:	(describe the position you seek)
Work Record: dates (from–to)	(in *reverse* chronological order) Company name Job title Major work functions and responsibilities Noteworthy accomplishments
Job-related Experience:	(any nonpaid work or experiences which may have contributed to the development of abilities relevant to your technical field)
Education:	(*reverse* chronological order) Degree, certificate, or diploma; date, name of institution, and brief synopsis of course of study; and special courses or accomplishments should be included.
Related Activities:	(include hobbies which relate to your field in some way and any special accomplishments)

Personal:
    (There is some disagreement among authorities about the importance of personal data—age, marital status, health, etc.—on the résumé.

Some feel it is helpful and of interest to a prospective employer while others feel it is contrary to Affirmative Action philosophy. The same kind of controversy surrounds the question of including a photograph with the résumé. Do what you feel is appropriate.)

References: Include name, title, company or institution, and phone number of the following:
One work reference
One school reference
One personal reference

Depending upon the kind of information you wish to include in your résumé, here are some other categories you may wish to use:

Military Record: Include year entered and year discharged, branch, specialized training, kinds of work and responsibilities involved. Special achievements (medals, etc.), exit rank, type of discharge, and reserve status should be included.

Licenses Earned or Certification: Include anything relevant to your work or indicative of your character.

Other Accomplishments (Honors or Awards): List work related competition, special recognitions, and the like.

Portfolio Available: For some fields (such as drafting, graphic arts, secretarial) it will be to your advantage to prepare a portfolio of samples of your work. If you have prepared a portfolio, it should be mentioned in the résumé.

Apprenticeship Record: Include the following information if appropriate:
1. Local Union number.
2. Institution in which you took your apprenticeship training
3. Your apprenticeship status

Affiliations: Mention membership in any professional or community organizations, unions, or societies. If relevant to a particular position you are seeking, include religious or political affiliations.

Availability: When can you start work?

Salary Desired: If you are just entering the field it is best to write "will negotiate."

GENERALLY ACCEPTED GUIDELINES WHICH YOU SHOULD FOLLOW IN PREPARING YOUR RÉSUMÉ:

1. Choose the general areas or categories of information you wish to include in your résumé. (These will be placed in the wide left-hand margin.) See the notes on "Format," pages 75 to 77. Then list the specific positions or experience in *reverse* chronological order. If the list is quite long, you might more effectively choose to put down first those experiences most relevant to the position you are applying for. Dates for each item listed are usually placed in the left-hand margin but indented slightly from the heading.

2. Each experience or past employment listed should include a short, clear description of your job and responsibilities. Emphasize those which are relevant to the new position you want.

3. The résumé should be neat, clear, and easy to read. Remember, employers file résumés for reference, and so the information contained in them should be easy to find or refer to at a glance. Use bold type, underlining, margins, and spacing to help focus on headings and divisions.

4. Language should be as accurate and brief as possible, omitting unnecessary words. The style of writing for résumés is unique: Sentences are choppy and abbreviated, transitions are eliminated, and punctuation is somewhat unconventional. Study the style in the sample résumés on pages 79 and 80.

5. Do not use abbreviations (particularly "etc.") or initials (e.g., I.V.T.C. for Indiana Vocational Technical College). Write out all terms and proper nouns.

6. At this point in your career you should be able to fit the information of your résumé on one or two pages. Number the bottom of the first page accordingly: "page 1 of 1" (or 2, etc., depending on the total number of pages in the résumé). Number the following pages in the same manner.

7. Use standard-size paper (8½" x 11") of good quality. Make sure the copy is perfect—free from any typographical errors, misspelling, or noticeable corrections. Remember to keep an attractive amount of "white space" by using one-inch margins, by double-spacing between paragraphs, and by using short paragraphs. Xeroxing is an acceptable method of duplication, but professionally printed résumés are most effective and usually inexpensive.

8. Use the minimum number of words necessary to convey accurately what you wish to say. Avoid introductory phrases such as "My responsibilities included" or "I graduated from . . ." Instead, start your sentences with the action words (listed below) that describe the main accomplishments you wish to convey to an employer, such as "Saved $500.00," "Designed a better system," or "Organized the parts department."

HOW TO SAY IT WITH ACTION

Certain words and phrases are helpful in writing an effective résumé. Study the following list of *action words* and notice how they may be used to phrase some of the important parts of your résumé.

Accustomed to dealing with/ operating/supervising	Organized
Active in	Participated in
Administered	Planned
Affiliated with	Prepared
Aided	Presented
Assumed responsibility for	Produced
Analyzed	Received diploma/degree/ certificate in
Assisted	Received recognition for
Conducted	Reduced costs
Contacted	Reorganized
Created	Researched
Designed	Served as president/director, etc.
Developed	Sold
Established	Studied
Evaluated	Supervised
Exhibited	Supported
Expanded	Taught
Experienced in operation of	Trained
Handled	Volunteered
Have working knowledge of	Was promoted
Held position in	Was associated with
Implemented	Was awarded/granted/cited/named
Improved	Was responsible to
Invented	Worked closely with engineer/ chief technician/physician
Maintained	
Managed	
Negotiated	
Operated	

Now observe how these words and phrases are applied to the major headings in your résumé.

Résumé of

ROBERT R. LIEBENSTROM
428 North Allison
Speedway, Indiana 46216

Social Security: 422-70-0963
Telephone: 635-9707

Job/Work Objective:	To be associated with a firm that has a large programming or computer department or is planning to install such a section to modernize and develop the firm. To work where technical background, imagination, mathematical skills, and writing ability can be fully used.
Personal Data	Single. Weight: 150 lbs. Height: 5'9". Good health.
Educational Record	Indiana Vocational Technical College Associate Degree 1974, Computer Technology, 3.0 grade average. Special emphasis on assembler language and Fortran programming. Related studies included 16 hours of accounting.

Experience

Part-time and Summers 1972-1974	Data Processing Information Service, Indianapolis, Indiana Data Processing Assistant. Worked in different departments of company before becoming general assistant in this major installation with all types of equipment and computers. Able to handle many different projects as contracted.
Part-time and Summers 1970-1972	Blocks Department Store, Speedway, Indiana Began as clerk; after one year worked as night manager. Took inventory, worked with buyer on ordering.
Part-time after school 1969-1970	Worked at my father's service station. Pumped gas, minor service--general assistant with a variety of duties.
Special Interests	Chess, tennis, bicycling, and local politics; reading technical periodicals.
References (By permission)	Mr. A. J. Thompson, Data Processing Instructor, Indiana Vocational Technical College, 1315 East Washington Street, Indianapolis, Indiana 635-6100
	Mr. W. T. Sutton, Assistant Director, Data Processing Information Services, 4898 East 34th Street, Indianapolis, Indiana 746-1686
	Mr. P. R. Renten, Assistant Manager, Blocks Department Store, 3586 South Madison Avenue, Indianapolis, Indiana 925-6801

Résumé

Hilde B. Johnson
266 Webster, N.E.   Social Security: 402-68-9220
Muncie, Indiana 46211   Telephone: (211) 368-5574

OCCUPATIONAL   Position as secretary-stenographer where training and ex-
OBJECTIVE   perience can be used in a variety of work responsibilities.

PERSONAL   Age 24, 5'6", 120 pounds. Excellent health. Married, no
DATA   children. Licensed public notary.

EXPERIENCE
HIGHLIGHTS

1971 to   Bobbs-Merrill Publishers, Indianapolis, Indiana
PRESENT   This firm specializes in distributing its own publications,
                    and some publications from European countries.

                    Secretary (full-time one year, part-time while in school).
                    Work as assistant in editor-in-chief's office. Take active
                    part in manuscript's final preparation before sending to
                    printers. Check for clear copy, spelling, grammar, typing,
                    to keep mistakes in proofs to a minimum.

1968 to   New Leaf Realty Company, Indianapolis, Indiana
1971   Secretary/receptionist. Responsible for handling or routing
                    phone calls and relaying detailed messages. Received
                    clients; maintained records, ad book, and files. Typed
                    business correspondence; was particularly concerned with
                    accuracy in typing real-tron cards for listings.

EDUCATION   IVTC 1973, Technician's Certificate in Secretarial Science.
                    Typing: 60 wpm. Stenography (Gregg): 120 rpm.

                    Richman High School, Trenton, N.J. High School diploma 1968.
                    Class Salutatorian.

ACTIVITIES   Volunteer for American Civil Liberties Union: type and do
                    some research. Interested in golf, travel, and crafts.

REFERENCES: Deanna Timmons, Instructor, Indiana Vocational Technical
(By permission)   College, 1315 East Washington Street, Indianapolis, Indiana,
                    635-6100

                    W. R. Raleigh, Editor-in-Chief, Bobbs-Merrill Co., 4300
                    West 62nd Street, Indianapolis, Indiana, 635-6801

                    Mr. John J. Browning, Realtor, 587 South Grand Street,
                    Indianapolis, Indiana, 545-6801

Education:

Received diploma/degree/certificate in _____.
Trained, studied _____.
Was awarded/granted/named_____.

Work Experience:

Was associated with _____. Sold _____.
Managed _____. Supervised _____.
Was promoted to _____.
Worked closely with_____.
Held position in _____.
Taught_____. Developed _____.
Assumed responsibility for_____.

Special Skills:

Have working knowledge of _____.
Experienced in operation of _____.
Created _____.
Designed _____.
Accustomed to dealing with/operating, etc._____.

Special Interests and Recognition:

Was cited/voted/elected _____.
Volunteered _____.
Active in _____.
Affiliated with _____.
Received recognition for _____.
Served as president/director/secretary_____.

COVER LETTERS

One of the most important pieces of material you will ever write about yourself is the personal cover letter you send out with every résumé. It is the ideal place to emphasize specific skills to an employer; in fact, the cover letter is like a personal introduction to a prospective employer. Here are some guidelines for writing a good cover letter:

1. The letter should be hand typed. It should be addressed specifically to the person (name and title) who will most likely be doing the interviewing for the job you have in mind. (Find out this information by calling the employer's switchboard.)

2. As in the résumé alternative, try to have your letter show that you know something about the problems and concerns of a particular company.

```
                                    127 Barclay Street
                                    Olympia, WA  98502
                                    (206) 843-2971



Dr. Warren Slaton, President
Seattle Community College
12 Rocky Mount Road
Seattle, WA  98101

Dear Dr. Slaton:

My experience on the administrative staffs of two colleges should be of interest
to you in your new drive to centralize administrative functions at SCC.

The enclosed resume will illustrate my ability to handle the specific adminis-
trative problems of a college department.

I am moving to Seattle at the end of the school year.  I will be in Seattle from
April 10-14.  If possible, I would like to arrange an appointment during that
period to discuss your new organization and how my experience could contribute
to your program.

                                    Very truly yours,


                                    Barbara Simon

Enc:  Resume
```

3. The cover letter should not run more than three or four paragraphs and should rarely be more than one page.

4. Always close with a request for an interview, suggesting a specific time.

5. As you prepare your cover letters, remember the rules of good writing and typing. Make letters short, to the point, and as interesting as possible. Remember, they will be viewed as samples of your writing skills.

6. Every time you mail a résumé and cover letter, be sure to make a record of it.

7. Finally, be sure to make a carbon copy of all the cover letters that you send out, and keep them for future reference.

PREPARING FOR THE JOB INTERVIEW

PURPOSE OF THE INTERVIEW

The purpose of a job interview for both you and your prospective employer is to exchange information and to provide a basis for judgment.

The interviewer usually has an idea in mind of the type of person he or she wishes to hire. For the interviewer, this is an opportunity to question you in an effort to see how you respond: the quality of your replies, your attitude, and your personality. The interviewer can match up an impression of you with an impression of the demands of the position to be filled. Are you really qualified? Will your past experience benefit the organization? Will you fit in with the rest of the team?

You have a fairly clear view of yourself but need to know about the specific position for which you are applying. The interview gives you an opportunity to find out more about what the job involves. What are its special demands? What is the work situation like? What sort of people would you be working for and with?

At the end of a successful interview *both* people should be able to tell if the job suits the applicant.

DOING YOUR "HOMEWORK" BEFORE THE INTERVIEW

Before applying for a particular position you will of course prepare your résumé and collect all the necessary data for filling out the application. However, these are only the first steps in preparing yourself for the interview. The brief job description in the classified ads or in another source should not be your sole motivation for applying for work. Favorite questions interviewers ask are: Why do you want to work for us? Do you know someone who works for the company? Are you familiar with its products or services? Have you read about it somewhere? Whatever the reason for your initial interest, it is a good idea to follow up by doing some research into the company.

When dealing with a small concern, you can sometimes get information from others in the community who are familiar with its operation and reputation. A large company will usually have some kind of public relations department (or director) you can contact for information. It is best to visit the place in person so you can follow up on questions and possibly get some literature or brochures prepared by the company about its services, products, and policies.

This kind of "homework" can help you prepare questions you will want to ask during the interview and will help you plan your answers to questions the interviewer might ask. Consequently you will be more likely to make a positive impression as an applicant and your time will have been well spent.

YOUR APPROACH TO THE INTERVIEW

Arrive a few minutes early. How you keep this appointment reflects directly on your punctuality. Allow extra time to get to the place of interview so you are not rushed. Hurrying unsettles your nerves and often affects your behavior.

If for a good reason you find you cannot keep the appointment, telephone the interviewer as far in advance as possible and ask to reschedule the interview.

Dress neatly and as you feel the interviewer might expect an employee to look. If you are applying for a medical position, a white uniform is often preferred, and your hair should be off the collar. (For women this means either cut short or pinned up.) Many employers do not like male applicants with long hair. You should be aware of this, and you may want to compromise your hair style slightly to increase your chances of being hired.

Do not bring anyone with you to the interview. You want to appear self-confident, not dependent on someone else for moral support. When you enter the office, behave normally and calmly. When it seems convenient to those present, explain who you are and why you have come. Try to look pleasant and wait for the interviewer to extend a hand or offer you a seat. (Place hat, coat, etc., on your lap or on the floor, not on the desk.)

FACE TO FACE

More often than not, a job is either clinched or lost on the basis of an interview. The interview gives you a chance to sell yourself—to reveal qualities which cannot be covered in a résumé. Keeping this in mind, let the interviewer lead the conversation. Listen carefully to the questions and stay to the point when you respond. Answer carefully and completely. You should be polite and confident. Above all keep any negative reactions or contrary opinions to yourself. During the interview watch for opportunities to ask questions of your own, particularly those about the company or the job. Do not ask about minor matters such as coffee breaks. Save any unanswered questions about salary range and fringe benefits until other aspects of the position have been covered.

In general, you should try to communicate to a prospective employer these three main points:

1. You are sincerely interested in the job and in the company.

2. Your training and experience are right for this particular position.

3. You have the kind of personality and intelligence which will fit in with the "team" and contribute positively to the company.

In most job interviews the interviewer will direct the course of talk and will ask specific questions. Brief yourself for this type of interview by preparing answers to questions such as the following:

1. *Why do you want to work here?* Now your company research pays off.

2. *Why did you leave your last position?* Keep your answer simple. Do not use your need for more money as your main reason. Perhaps you saw no opportunity for advancement or challenge, or your position may have been eliminated. Another reason for leaving might be that you wished to find work more relevant to recent training. Whatever your reasons, emphasize the positive rather than the negative aspects. For example, instead of saying "I just didn't like my old job" you might say "I wanted to find a position where I could apply my training to a greater extent."

3. *Why do you feel you are especially suited to this type of work?* This open question could be asking about your technical qualifications and/or aspects of your personality. Your answer should include both kinds of reasons, and should be well thought out in advance.

4. *What kind of salary do you feel you should have?* (or more directly: what do you think you are worth?) Before going into the interview you should find out what the salary range is for this type of position. Then consider your present or more recent salary along with any projected increase justified by:

(a) recent training or experience

(b) increased responsibility in the position for which you are applying

After thinking over your situation, set a salary range for what you feel you can expect. When the question of salary comes up, ask for the higher end of your range and be able to justify it. If it is more than the company expects to pay, you should be prepared to take less. Then the company can feel it is getting a bargain. If you should ask for less than the job pays, you may be thought of as not worth the established salary minimum. Any company likes to feel it gets full value for its salary dollar.

OTHER INTERVIEW QUESTIONS FOR WHICH YOU SHOULD BE PREPARED

Think through answers and explanations for each of the following. Rehearse them in your mind.

1. What qualities or qualifications make you feel that you will be successful in this field?

2. Why did you choose the school where you received your training?

3. Do you think you could forget your training and learn a new system?

4. Are you looking for part-time or full-time work? Temporary or permanent?

5. What have you learned from the experience you have had? How does it relate to the position here?

6. How do you get along with other people? Any trouble with supervisors before?

7. What type of people do you find most difficult to get along with?

8. What personal characteristics do you feel are necessary to succeed in this field?

9. What do you feel is your major weakness? What do others feel is your major weakness?

10. What do you see as the disadvantages of working in this field?

11. Which jobs have you enjoyed the most? The least? Why?

12. What have you done which shows you have the initiative or willingness to work?

13. How do you feel about overtime work? Moving to another area?

14. What would your ambitions be if you worked for this company?

15. What do you plan to be doing five years from now? Ten years from now?

SOME OTHER CONSIDERATIONS

Some interviewers favor interviews where the applicant does most of the talking. In this type of interview the interviewer may open with a broad question such as "Tell me about yourself," expecting you to take the lead, to supply all the relevant information about yourself and to ask questions about the job. If you should find yourself in this kind of situation, it is always helpful to begin by explaining your interest in the company and in the position for which you are applying. Then after asking specific questions about the nature of the job and its responsibilities, you can go on to show how your training and experience could benefit the company.

Occasionally you may run across an employer who is unskilled at interviewing or who tends to wander off the point. If that happens, you can steer the conversation back by saying something like "I'm really very interested in (*company's name*), Mr. Jones, and in the possibility of working here and if I may, I'd like to find out a little more about just what the job involves . . ." or ". . . to explain to you why I believe I'm qualified for this job . . ."

In any interview your speech is important. Using poor grammar or slang would spoil the effect you would like to make. Language is particularly important for those entering any of the business fields. Shyness in answering questions may be interpreted as indifference. On the other hand, too much aggressiveness and an "I can do anything" approach will also make a bad impression. The brief encounter during the interview may be your only chance to prove that you as a person are better for the job than any other applicant.

The interview is probably the most competitive aspect of the whole job application process. If you keep this in mind, prepare carefully, and accomplish the three main points mentioned earlier, you should be able to consider your interview a successful one.

GOODBYE AND AFTER

After talking to you, your interviewer may tell you that your qualifications are unsuitable for the position. Or the interviewer may say that you will be considered along with several other applicants and that he or she will let you know of the decision. Then again you may be fortunate enough to be offered the job at the close of the interview. In any case you should thank the interviewer for the time and say goodbye politely and promptly.

Regardless of the outcome of the interview, you should think it over carefully and separate the strengths from the weaknesses in your self-presentation.

If you should be fortunate enough to receive more than one job offer as a result of your interviews, in making a decision keep in mind your long-range goals. Salary should not be your sole motivation in accepting one position over another. Consider the following:

1. Opportunity for advancement and challenge

2. Opportunity for continuing your education while you work

3. The effect this particular job may have on future plans

4. Specific working conditions

5. Fringe benefits

You may realize after analyzing these points that the job offering the lowest beginning pay would be the best choice for this first stage of your long-range plan.

Whatever decisions you make, be sure to keep the door open. If you are informed that you have not been hired, you may politely ask the reason. Was it a matter of experience? Training? In any case thank the interviewer and ask him/her to keep your application on file in case a position appropriate for you might open up in the future.

Should you decide to accept a particular job offer after several interviews, you should inform the other employers of your decision as soon as possible.

Most of the material in this chapter was taken from "Marketing Your Occupational Skills," a mini-course written by Lynne DeMichele and tested at Indiana Vocational Technical College, Indianapolis. The course was developed through the Indiana State Board of Vocational/Technical Education with funds from a federal education grant.

The material on "Your Résumé—What It Is" (pages 73-75) was taken from "Project: Résumé—A Dynamic, New Approach to Spotlighting Your Abilities," by Laura Terrone (Today's Secretary, March 1977, page 7).

UNIT 6

The Library Research Paper

CONTENTS

LEARNING OBJECTIVE

•To select an appropriate topic for a research paper

An appropriate topic has the following characteristics:

1. The topic should be of interest to the writer.

2. The intended reader should approve of the selection of the topic as an appropriate subject for a research paper.

3. An adequate number of resources for research should be available.

4. The topic should be properly limited to the space at your disposal. Obviously, you cannot adequately cover a subject as broad as "the population explosion" in a ten-page research paper. In the following examples, note how a topic can be limited for treatment in compositions of various lengths:

Virtually unlimited: "Computer Science"

Limited for book length: "Applications of Computer Science in Medicine"

Limited for research paper length: "New Applications of Computer Science in Radiology"

Limited for research paper length: "The Use of the Computer in Keeping Medical Records"

Always select a topic appropriate to your purpose for writing. Ask yourself what your principal objective is. You should write a clear statement of purpose before beginning your essay; it may be helpful to think in terms of one of the following basic types of writing:

1. *Exposition* (to inform)
   Sample purpose statement: "The computer is currently used by most large hospitals for keeping medical records."

2. *Argument* (to persuade)
   Sample purpose statement: "Public hospitals should provide at-cost access to computers for diagnosis."

3. *Description* (to convey a sensory impression—usually visual)
   Sample purpose statement: "The fourth-generation computers will look considerably different than current ones."

4. *Narration* (to present events or steps in a particular time sequence)
   Sample purpose statement: "Processing a blood sample through a computer for analysis proceeds according to a careful plan."

Remember: Your statement of purpose will be the controlling idea of your paper. As such it should be made final only after you carefully limit your topic and choose an approach. Ideally, it should be a complete sentence containing a subject (your topic) and a verb or object (the attitude or approach you have chosen in regard to the topic).

If you select a subject relevant to your chosen field, current trade and technical publications contain information on the latest developments in a given area—always fertile ground for a research topic. Consider investigating some new application of an established technology, a new technical procedure, a new product or type of equipment, or a discussion of some new trend.

Following is a list of possible topics related to various technical careers. Each of these topics might be developed in a number of ways. Remember, once you select a subject, you must narrow it to a scope appropriate for your paper. Then you should develop from it a clear statement of purpose.

Electronics	Citizens' Band Radios
	Video Disc Systems
	The Laser
	Medical Electronics
Automotive	The Mazda Engine
	Future Fuel Alternatives
	Environmental Protection Agency Standards
	The Three-Wheeled Car
Heating and air conditioning	The Heat Pump
	Freon

	Solar Energy
	Air Conditioning in Agricultural Equipment
Drafting	Laminated Wood Beam Construction
	Blueprint Copyrighting
	Computers in Design
	The Geodesic Dome
Construction	Ferro-cement
	Suboceanic Construction
	Problems of Prefabrication
	The Modular Home
Allied health	The Private Nursing Practice
	Malpractice Insurance for Medical Technicians
	Dealing with Death
	The Annual Health Checkup
Police science	Anticipating the Crime
	Ballistic Science
	Hostage Crimes
	Special Weapons and Tactical Forces
Business	Computer Time Sharing
	Certification for Secretaries
	Tax Accountants
	Stock Options
	Management by Objectives

LEARNING OBJECTIVE

•To prepare a working bibliography

After you have selected an appropriate topic, you are ready to begin preparing a bibliography which will list all the sources of information to be used in writing your paper.

The most helpful place to begin searching for sources is the card catalog of your library, for it usually lists all books and bound magazines owned by your institution. Other library tools which may be helpful in locating sources of information include the *Reader's Guide,* the vertical file, and reference books such as dictionaries, encyclopedias, and atlases. Your librarian will be glad to direct you to these tools and to explain how to use them.

Whenever you find a book or an article which looks promising, record complete information on the source on a separate 3" x 5" or 4" x 6" index card. The information on each card should follow precisely the bibliographical form you have been directed to use by your instructor. The form used on the card that follows and in the model bibliographical entries in this unit is based on the *Style Sheet* of the Modern Language Association. (Notice that the card catalog call number is conveniently located in the upper left-hand corner.)

```
HT
151
.G53
        Gist, Noel P., and Sylvia Fleis Fava.
            Urban Society. New York:  Thomas
            W. Crowell Company, 1974.
```

LEARNING OBJECTIVE

·To formulate an appropriate outline

1. First scan the table of contents and the various headings of every resource in your preliminary working bibliography. This will give you a general idea of the topics your paper might include.

2. Second, jot down a list of ideas and topics you hope to develop within the scope of your paper. After completing the list, carefully remove any topics which do not seem to be related to the central idea (or purpose) of your intended composition.

3. Third, pick out those ideas which will become the main points of your paper. Then write in subordinate points and details for each in outline form, taking care to organize in a clear and logical manner.

4. For the fourth step you should reexamine your purpose statement to see if your outline does indeed accomplish that purpose. You may find it necessary to fill in some gaps or possibly even readjust your purpose statement.

Most students find the informal "topic outline" easiest to use as a framework for composition. Note in the example below how a single word or a short phrase is used for each point.

THE TOPIC OUTLINE

Purpose Statement: **When one recognizes the relationship of unlimited population and economic growth to environmental problems, several possible solutions suggest themselves.**

I.   Population and the problems of urban areas
   A.   Pollution
   B.   Overcrowded public facilities

II. Continued migration to urban areas
    A. Census reports
    B. Los Angeles smog control efforts
III. Population growth and economic expansion
    A. High standard of living
    B. High levels of energy waste
IV. Possible Solutions
    A. Galbraith and Mishan's theories
    B. Change of life-style

CHECK LIST FOR OUTLINES

1. The parts of the outline must be arranged in a logical sequence.
2. The outline should adequately cover the subject specifically suggested by the purpose statement.
3. Check for informational balance: Are major headings of equal weight or importance? Are they all clearly tied to the purpose statement? Is there a consistent level of information among subheadings?
4. Use one system of notation and indent subheadings to indicate degrees of subordination, as in the guide that follows:
    I. Used for major headings
       A. Used for first-degree subheadings
       B. Used for first-degree subheadings
          1. Used for second-degree subheadings
          2. Used for second-degree subheadings

Note: **Rarely does an outline need to go beyond second-degree subheadings. If it does, use a., b., c., etc., for the third degree and (1), (2), (3), etc., for the fourth degree.**

5. Do not allow single headings or subheadings to appear in the outline. Any heading implies a division into at least two parts. If there is a I, there should be a II; if there is an A, there should be a B; and so forth.
6. Remember that you may need to revise your outline several times before your research is complete. In other words, your first outline will be only a preliminary outline. As you read and take notes, your preliminary outline will probably be altered several times, and your final outline will not emerge until the final draft of your paper is written.

LEARNING OBJECTIVE
•To take effective notes

1. Before you proceed with your reading and notetaking, you should try to check the reliability of your sources by asking the following questions:
    (a) Is the author a recognized authority on the subject?
    (b) What is the copyright date? In many technical areas some information is out of date in less than five years.
    (c) Does the author seem to be prejudiced about the subject matter? Is his

or her view limited by personal background? For example, an electronics engineer may analyze a new medical diagnostic instrument but is not in a position to evaluate its use in actual medical procedure.

(d) Are your magazine and newspaper articles taken from recent sources that are authoritative and dependable?

2. As you gain experience in reading and in taking notes, you will learn how to locate the most helpful information without wasting time. Only rarely will you need to read an entire book or article to find pertinent subject matter. The following suggestions will help you save time.

(a) Check the table of contents and the subject matter index to help locate specific information.

(b) Scan the various headings (often in boldface print).

(c) Learn to spot topic sentences, "clincher" sentences, and summarizing statements.

3. After your preliminary outline is complete, you are ready to begin reading your sources and taking notes. The notes you take will be for the purpose of developing each topic or subtopic in your outline. It is suggested that you use note cards rather than sheets of paper, as information can be sorted and organized more easily. At the top of each card jot down the outline topic (Part I, II, etc.) developed by the note on that particular card. Directly below the outline topic, write complete footnote information according to the form you have been directed to use by your instructor.

If you will be using many footnotes, it may be more convenient to keep one numbered list of sources containing all the necessary bibliographical information. Then as you take notes, put a number in the upper right-hand corner of each card keyed to the appropriate entry on your source list.

4. One of the most common errors in taking notes is copying too many direct quotations. Generally, too many quotations indicate that you have not adequately understood the material. You are expected to gather information and ideas from your sources and write them in your own words. The reason for this is simple: If you copy the words of another writer, you are not gaining experience in composition. However, you may quote whenever you find a passage that is so important and so well phrased that it would strengthen your paper or add emphasis. Remember that a direct quotation should always be copied verbatim (word for word), enclosed in quotation marks, and footnoted properly.

LEARNING OBJECTIVE
·To use footnotes when appropriate

Students are frequently confused about what should be footnoted and what should not be footnoted. Actually, it is impossible to draw up a set of definite rules by which you can always determine when a footnote is necessary. If you are writing on a subject that is quite new to you, it may seem at first glance that you will need a footnote for almost every sentence in your paper. But this will not be necessary if you have properly digested the material and used your own words. (*Hint:* In most instances when you "digest" material you are compressing it into fewer words.) Nevertheless, there are a number of situations in which you must always use a footnote:

1. All direct quotations must be footnoted. Even when you quote only part of a sentence, you should acknowledge the quote with a footnote. If several phrases or single words are quoted and combined with your own words, it is not always necessary to footnote each individual quote. For example, you could have a sentence similar to the following:

> On July 13, 1863, the Confederate forces constructed individual "breastworks," built "train traps," and prepared to "stem the tide of battle."

In such a sentence it would not be necessary to footnote each interior quote. Instead, the footnote would be placed at the end of the sentence.

If you are quoting a long passage—one consisting of more than one hundred words—you should single-space the quote and set it off an additional half-inch on each side. The single-spacing and extra indention are enough to indicate that the passage is a quotation, and quotation marks are not used. A footnote is placed at the end of the quoted material.

2. All paraphrases must be footnoted. A paraphrase is another writer's idea expressed in your own words. The fact that you have altered the wording does not make the idea your own. A good paraphrase is usually shorter than the material being paraphrased.

3. A footnote should also be used whenever you summarize several pages in a source, no matter how completely the words of the summary may be your own.

4. Occasionally, a footnote may be used to define a special term or to clarify highly specialized or technical information.

5. On rare occasions two different sources will disagree and a footnote may be used to call attention to the disagreement and to clarify the relationship of various points (coherence).

6. The writer of a research paper may want to call attention to a segment of content that has come before or that will come later in his paper. In such cases the writer may use footnotes to refer the reader to other sections of the paper.

Note: **If what you are writing is going to be published, in many cases you**

will need written permission to quote from published sources. In this case, be sure you have whatever permissions are necessary.

On the other hand, there are two fairly clear instances in which you do not need a footnote.

1. Any information which is so much a part of you that you can write about it freely without referring to your notes or to any printed page has become your own knowledge and does not usually require a footnote.

Caution: **If you should choose to incorporate highly specialized information based on your own knowledge, it may be necessary to refer in a footnote to some established source where that information may be found in order to establish its validity. Exceptions to this might be cases in which your training or education qualify you as an authority on a given area of information.**

2. Facts which are common knowledge do not require a footnote. For instance, you do not need to refer to a source to state that Columbus arrived in North America in 1492 or that Pearl Harbor was attacked on December 7, 1941.

Caution: **Do not be guilty of plagiarism. If you fail to footnote any ideas you have borrowed or any passages you have quoted directly, you are plagiarizing. To avoid this, take great care to use your own words and your own sentence structure and follow carefully the procedure for proper footnoting.**

LEARNING OBJECTIVE

•To write the first draft of your research paper

1. After you have taken notes on every topic in your outline, you are ready to begin organizing your note cards. Assemble the cards according to the outline topics. In other words, each topic in your outline should be supported by the information on one or more note cards. This simple task of stacking the cards according to topic or subtopic goes a long way toward organizing your paper.

2. Second, begin writing the first draft of the paper by referring to the information on your note cards. Take one topic or subtopic at a time (by referring to one stack of cards at a time) and develop it adequately. You may discover that some of your topics or subtopics can be eliminated. Others may be expanded.

3. One of the most important tasks in writing the first draft is providing transitional sentences and possibly even transitional paragraphs. Examples of these transitional devices are underlined in the model research paper at the end of this unit. The primary purpose of a transitional device is to keep your thoughts flowing smoothly from one section of your paper to another.

4. Remember to insert consecutive numbers (e.g., 1, 2, 3, 4, etc.) at each point where a footnote is necessary.

LEARNING OBJECTIVE
·To write the final draft of your research paper

The following checklist is provided to help you in writing your final draft:

1. Your first draft is the most important step in creating a superior final draft. After your first draft is complete, go back and read it word by word and letter by letter. Your goal will be 100 percent accuracy in form and mechanics.

2. Look up every word about which you have the slightest doubt of the correct spelling.

3. Analyze the grammatical construction of each sentence to be certain that every punctuation mark is in its proper place.

4. Based on the topic sentence, is each paragraph unified, coherent, and adequately developed?

5. Are transitional devices included to provide a smooth flow of thought?

6. Do your margins and typing specifications meet the requirements of your instructor?

7. Have you remembered to include all periods and commas *inside* closing quotation marks? This is one of the most frequent errors students commit.

8. Have you achieved 100 percent accuracy of form in your footnotes and bibliography?

9. If required by your instructor, have you included a title page, an outline, a statement of purpose, or a concluding statement?

10. Finally, does your paper look neat? Neatness and attention to detail are extremely important when conducting research.

LEARNING OBJECTIVE
·Using correct form in writing footnotes

Footnotes are usually typed at the bottom of the page on which they are used. When you have determined how much space you will need at the bottom of a given page, you should type a short line (about two inches long) two spaces below the last line on the page. This line extends from the left margin toward the center of the page. Your footnotes should begin two spaces below this line.

As an alternative method, some instructors allow their students to type all footnotes on one or more pages at the end of the paper. (This is the style that the MLA recommends.) When this procedure is followed, place the footnote page or pages immediately following the final page of content and place the bibliography page after the footnotes.

The first line of each footnote entry should be indented five spaces. Remember that footnotes are generally numbered consecutively throughout the paper, and each number appears a half space above the first line of each entry. (See the sample paper at the end of this unit.)

When the same source is used a second time, you may use the Latin abbreviation *Ibid.* (meaning "in the same place") for the second footnote on a manuscript page. When you start a new page, you should not use *Ibid.*, but rather use the author's last name, an abbreviated title, and page numbers. The abbreviated title may be omitted if only one work by a given author is referred to in your paper and if the complete reference is easily found in a recent footnote. Observe the following examples:

[1]Desmond Morris, *The Human Zoo* (New York: McGraw-Hill Book Company, 1969), p. 73.

[2]*Ibid.*, pp. 80-82.

[3]Morris, pp. 85-87.

In this instance footnote 3 uses "Morris" instead of another *Ibid.* because footnote 3 (in the actual paper) is located on the page after footnote 2. If more than one book by the same author is cited in the footnotes, it is necessary to use an abbreviated title as well as the author's last name.

As you type your footnotes, notice that the author's first name is always listed first. Commas followed by only one space are used to separate the major divisions of a footnote entry. An exception to this separation by comma rule would be a question mark or an exclamation point coming at the end of an article title, a situation that occurs in footnote 7 of the sample paper. Remember, footnotes are supposed to be sentences, and they are punctuated accordingly.

SAMPLE FOOTNOTE ENTRIES

A book with a single author

[1]Alvin Toffler, *Future Shock* (New York: Random House, Inc., 1970), pp. 203-205.

A book with two or three authors

[2]Kenneth L. Jones, Louis W. Shainberg, and Curtis O. Byer, *Drugs, Alcohol, and Tobacco* (San Francisco: Canfield Press, 1970), pp. 21-23.

If a book has more than three authors, you should cite only the first author listed and use the Latin abbreviation *et al.* to represent the remaining authors.

An article from a newspaper

[3]Edward Downes, "The Choral Singer Is a Dedicated Soul," *New York Times,* 27 January 1964, Section 2, p. 17, col. 3.

Whenever possible, it is helpful to include the column number (use col. or cols.).

Magazine articles

[4]"Dangerous Oversight," *Newsweek,* 12 March 1963, p. 29.

[5]John Ciardi, "Poetry in Three Dimensions," *Saturday Review,* 20 April 1964, pp. 22-23.

An article from a journal with continuous pagination throughout the annual volume

[6]Solomon H. Tilles, "An Experimental Approach to the Spanish American Theatre," *The Modern Language Journal,* 56 (May 1972), 304-305.

Notice that *Vol.* (before 56) and *pp.* (before 304-305) are omitted when both volume and page numbers are given. If pagination is continuous, the issue number is unnecessary.

An article from a journal which pages each issue separately

[7]Glen V. Ramsey, "The Emerging Volunteer," *Mental Hygiene,* 56, No. 2 (Spring 1972), 44-47.

As in the previous example *Vol.* and *pp.* are omitted when both volume and page numbers are given. However, since the pagination is *not* continuous through the volume, you must indicate which issue (No. 2) you are citing.

A signed encyclopedia article

[8]Richard Mercer Dorson, "Manifest Destiny," *Encyclopaedia Britannica,* 1971.

Note: Encyclopedia articles are often signed only with initials. Look up the full name in the bibliographical material in either Volume I or the last volume.

An unsigned encyclopedia article

[9]"Marchand, Jean Baptiste," *Encyclopaedia Britannica,* 1971.

A pamphlet

[10]*About the Ford Foundation* (New York: Ford Foundation Office of Reports, September 1968), p. 10.

A *personal interview*

[11]Richard B. Kline, electronics engineer, ConVac Corporation, information obtained from an interview on March 5, 1977.

LEARNING OBJECTIVE
•*Preparing a final bibliography according to correct form*

1. The first step is to stack your bibliography cards alphabetically according to the author's last name. If no author is given, you should alphabetize according to the first word in the title. The introductory words *A*, *An*, and *The* are disregarded whenever you alphabetize by title.

2. Remember that your final bibliography will include only those resources which were actually helpful in writing your paper—generally those which were cited in your footnotes. If you read a resource for background knowledge but did not cite it in your footnotes, some authorities feel it may be legitimately listed in your bibliography; since there is disagreement on this point, however, you should follow the preference of your instructor. When you have removed the cards containing resources you did not use, you are ready to begin typing your final bibliography.

3. The word BIBLIOGRAPHY or WORKS CONSULTED should be centered about two inches from the top of your bibliography page. Four spaces below the title you should enter your first resource.

4. The first line of each entry should begin flush with the left margin and all succeeding lines (of individual entries) should be indented five spaces from the left margin. The lines of each bibliography entry are single-spaced. Double-space between entries. Remember that bibliography entries are not numbered.

5. In the sample bibliography entries that follow, notice that the name of the first author listed (for each entry) is reversed so that the entire list may be alphabetized.

6. Remember, each piece of information in a bibliography entry is a separate statement. Punctuate accordingly.

SAMPLE BIBLIOGRAPHY ENTRIES

A *book with a single author*

Chase, Stuart. *The Most Probable World.* New York: Harper and Row, 1968.
When your bibliography entry is a book, you should place a period after the author's name and after the title of the book. Notice that two typing spaces

follow each of these periods. The colon after the place of publication should also be followed by two typing spaces.

A book with two or more authors

Ehrlich, Paul R., and Anne H. Ehrlich. *Population, Resources, Environment: Issues in Human Ecology.* San Francisco: W. H. Freeman, 1970.

Notice that the first name is reversed for alphabetizing. The second name is not reversed. If a book has three authors, neither the second name nor the third name is reversed. If a book has more than three authors, list only the name of the first author and use *et al.* as a substitute for the remaining authors.

A book compiled by an editor

Freedman, Ronald, ed. *Population: The Vital Revolution.* Garden City, New York: Doubleday and Company, 1964.

If more than one editor is involved, their names should be listed according to the instructions for two or more authors. Immediately following their names the abbreviation *eds.* may be used for the word *editors.*

A journal article

McAllister, Jerome, Sallie Cowgill, and Janith Stephenson. "Why Aren't Your Children Learning?" *Junior College Journal,* 42, No. 6 (March 1972), 24-25.

A period and two spaces follow the name of the author or authors of a journal article. Remember that the abbreviations *Vol.* and *pp.* are not used when both volume and page numbers are given.

A magazine article

"From Sea to Shining Sea." *Newsweek,* 75, No. 4 (26 January 1970), 36.

When the author's name is not given for a magazine article, the divisions of the entry may be separated by commas. If the author's name is given, it should appear before the title of the article and it should be followed by a period and two typing spaces. Remember to reverse the name for alphabetizing purposes.

A newspaper article

Jackson, Mark L. "Asks Blockade of Red China." *The Raleigh Times,* 27 November 1961, Section 4, p. 3.

If the author of a newspaper article is unknown, begin the entry with the first word of the article title.

A signed encyclopedia article

Dorson, Richard Mercer. "Manifest Destiny." *Encyclopaedia Britannica,* 1971.

F[rench], J[ohn] C. "Norris, Benjamin Franklin." *Dictionary of American Biography,* 1934.

When an encyclopedia article is signed with initials and you must look up the full name, use brackets for the parts of the name you looked up.

An unsigned encyclopedia article

"Marchand, Jean Baptiste." *Encyclopaedia Britannica,* 1971.

A pamphlet

About the Ford Foundation. New York: Ford Foundation Office of Reports, September 1968.

A personal interview

Kline, Richard B., electronics engineer, ConVac Corporation. Information obtained from an interview, March 5, 1977.

SAMPLE RESEARCH PAPER

This research paper was prepared by an English student. Discuss its strengths and weakness with your instructor. Underlined sentences are transitional, and the second paragraph is a transitional paragraph.

PEOPLE: BOTH THE PROBLEM AND THE SOLUTION

FOR OUR THREATENED ENVIRONMENT

by

Thomas A. Smith

English 102
Assistant Professor Ruth Merritt
May 9, 19--

PEOPLE: BOTH THE PROBLEM AND THE SOLUTION

FOR OUR THREATENED ENVIRONMENT

<u>Purpose Statement</u>: When one recognizes the relationship of unlimited
population and economic growth to environmental
problems, several possible solutions suggest
themselves.

The 1970 census reported that the population of the United States had

reached 204,765,770.[1] Does this mean that we are a seriously overpopulated

country? Unlike many other nations, we produce large quantities of goods and

we do not have a serious food shortage. Our natural resources could sustain

our present population for many years to come. Vast areas of land seem to be

uninhabited. It is tempting, therefore, to conclude that we do not have urgent

population problems in the United States.

It would be a tragic mistake, however, to believe that our population

growth has not caused serious environmental problems, particularly in urban

areas. These problems relate to pollution and to overuse of our public

facilities.

Consider the following: (1) In an inner-city neighborhood in Washington,

D.C., 25 percent of the children tested showed dangerously high levels of lead

in their blood. The source was not only lead-based house paint (which children

eat) but also lead-laden car exhaust fumes.[2] (2) School children in many of our

large cities may not take physical education classes outdoors on days of heavy

smog so that they do not breathe too deeply of the poisonous air. (3)

---

[1]United States Department of Commerce, Bureau of the Census, "Final 1970
Census Figures," <u>Commerce News</u> (press release), 1970.

[2]Colman McCarthy, "Will We Let Pollution Nibble Us to Death?" <u>Reader's
Digest</u>, 101, No. 604 (August 1972), 76.

Contamination of our water supply by industrial wastes is an ongoing threat
to our national health and affects our fish and plant life as well. (4) Public
utilities, some of which are extremely hazardous to clean air and water, are
overused, and major power failures occur often in some cities. (5) Traffic
congestion during peak commuter hours, when the exhaust fumes visibly contaminate
the air, remains unrelieved by new highway construction programs. (6) Recre-
ational facilities of all kinds are so crowded that we have become accustomed
to long lines and litter. All these environmental problems are compounded where
the population is concentrated.

Our population continues to drift toward urban centers, thereby worsening
the problems caused by overcrowding. The "big city's" opportunities and glamor
compensate for its many inconveniences, it seems. In 1790 most North Americans
lived in rural areas, but by 1975 three out of every four of us were living in
urban areas.[3] The 1970 census revealed that sixty-three of sixty-six of our
largest metropolitan areas registered gains over the 1960 census.[4] In other
words, our large urban areas are continuing to grow at a time when they are
already overcrowded.

This overcrowding nullifies attempts at reducing current environmental
problems. Not only does it worsen the difficulties of already overloaded
public facilities, but it also increases existing levels of pollution. In many
places air pollution in large urban centers--perhaps the most publicized of
environmental problems--has begun to affect surrounding areas also.

---

[3]Robert C. Cook and Jane Lecht, People: An Introduction to the Study of
Population (Washington, D.C.: Columbia Books, Population Reference Bureau,
1968), p. 51.

[4]United States Department of Commerce, Bureau of the Census, "Most of
Nation's Large Metropolitan Areas Show Gains Over 1960," Commerce News (press
release), 10 September 1970.

For example, in Los Angeles strict regulations and rigorous standards of enforcement by the County Air Pollution Control District have failed to reduce the level of smog; the volume of heavily polluted air is actually increasing. The deadly smog is spreading in area and in height; reportedly, air pollution is damaging plant life hundreds of miles to the east of Los Angeles.[5]

More people living in the same areas, occupying the same space, will produce more smog. The best one can do is keep the pollution levels steady despite the population growth. In the foreseeable future Los Angeles will keep its smog.

Not only is population growth a major factor in our increasing environmental problems, but it also urges on indefinite and unrestrained economic expansion. Such economic expansion, based on a steady increase in the use of energy from limited natural resources, is in itself another prime cause of current environmental problems. With the national emphasis on consumable goods, often produced at the expense of the environment, our standard of living continues to rise materially, while the quality of our life degenerates.

Modern technology is developing at a staggering rate in an effort to keep up with an ever-increasing demand for more advanced industrial production. This results in cars, machinery, and appliances, when what we now need are improved living conditions. A new crock-pot which requires thousands of worker-hours to devise, produce, and sell also produces more industrial waste to pollute our air and water and consumes even more of our valuable natural energy. Without self-imposed limits, not only does our economic growth cause environmental problems that harm us physically, but market demands also reduce the amount of

---

[5]Paul K. Ehrlich and Anne H. Ehrlich, Population, Resources, Environment: Issues in Human Ecology (San Francisco: W. H. Freeman, 1970), pp. 124-126.

[6]Ibid.

capital available that could be used to support programs for environmental protection and enhancement.

In seeking solutions to these problems, economists such as John Kenneth Galbraith and Ezra Mishan believe that the current emphasis on increased production of consumable goods must shift to an emphasis on the preservation of the quality of the environment in urban areas. Galbraith and Mishan would improve the quality of the city's physical facilities--sewage and water treatment plants, roads, parks, playgrounds, slum clearance--and would support the city's cultural facilities--schools, theaters, symphony orchestras, museums--with higher taxes. Theoretically, when people are heavily taxed, they cannot buy expensive automobiles, boats, air-conditioners, and other items that place a strain on our resources. Galbraith and Mishan argue that the GNP and per capita income can continue to rise for many years without adversely affecting the environment and society as long as the GNP is simultaneously shifted to services (the arts, education, recreation, public services) and a greater share of the increased revenue is spent on the control of pollution.[8]

The difficulty with Galbraith and Mishan's plans lies in their overlooking certain basic American freedoms. They may think the quality of life is better when you have an orchestra playing specially commissioned music in a public park, while someone else may prefer hot-rod racing on a dirt track. Who can decide which tax dollar is better spent?

Another more radical, solution to our urban problems involves a change in American attitude, specifically a willingness to accept a different standard of living. Our urban environmental problems may be partially explained by the

---

[7]Rufus E. Miles, Jr., "Whose Baby Is the Population Problem?" Population Bulletin, 16 (February 1970), 9.

[8]Miles, p. 11.

majority of our population's expecting a high standard of living. As a result,
we continue to demand that our factories produce goods which are luxuries to the
rest of the world. We build smog-producing cars to satisfy our urges for status
and speed; we destroy agricultural acreage to build split-level homes outside
the cities; we manufacture millions of indestructible plastic, metal, and glass
objects; we devour forests to make paper plates and books. If another fifty
million people are added to our present urban population, and if those fifty
million people demand the standard of living that currently exists, we may
completely destroy our living environment in urban areas.

We must learn to accept a different way of life. Some of the books we
produce already teach us how to live a simpler, less materialistic, less
destructive life. Many people, especially of the younger generation, have
come to realize that their wealth would be better spent on health rather than
on possessions. Happiness could be watching an avocado seed grow rather than
arranging bunches of fake grapes in a bowl. Already our population has
stopped expanding. For those generations to come we ought to leave a country
as plentiful and prosperous--and, if possible, more beautiful--as we enjoy at
present.

6

BIBLIOGRAPHY

Cook, Robert C., and Jane Lecht. <u>People</u>: <u>An Introduction to the Study of</u> <u>Population</u>. Washington, D.C.: Columbia Books, Population Reference Bureau, 1968.

Ehrlich, Paul R., and Anne H. Ehrlich. <u>Population, Resources, Environment</u>: <u>Issues in Human Ecology</u>. San Francisco: W. H. Freeman, 1970.

"Final 1970 Census Figures." <u>Commerce News</u> (press release), Washington, D.C.: United States Department of Commerce, Bureau of the Census, 1970.

McCarthy, Colman. "Will We Let Pollution Nibble Us to Death?" <u>Reader's Digest</u>, 101, No. 604 (August 1972), 76.

Miles, Rufus E., Jr. "Whose Baby Is the Population Problem?" <u>Population</u> <u>Bulletin</u>, 16 (February 1970), 4.

"Most of Nation's Large Metropolitan Areas Show Gains Over 1960." <u>Commerce</u> <u>News</u> (press release), Washington, D.C.: United States Department of Commerce, Bureau of the Census, 10 September 1970.

Part Two

UNIT 7

Basic Sentence Patterns

Every automobile mechanic is familiar with the parts of an engine, and also knows that each part must work properly and be installed correctly if the engine is to run smoothly. When something goes wrong with the car, the mechanic will check each part's performance against the manufacturer's specification manual. If the part is defective, the mechanic goes to the parts department and requests a replacement.

Similarly, a chapter on grammar is a *sentence* specification manual, for it describes the way our language works. If you know the various parts of a sentence and understand how these parts are put together in meaningful combinations, you will be able to improve your writing and speaking skills.

Employers and customers will expect correct grammar from you. For instance, what would a customer think if he asked to see a certain type of citizen's band radio and you told him that "We don't got none"? What would your employer think if you sent him a memo full of grammatical errors? Right or wrong, the occupational world demands employees who can use the tools of grammar to communicate accurately and correctly.

The examples that follow will show you the normal word order of the basic sentence patterns. Below each example a guide provides chapter and page references for the discussion of the different parts used to build each basic sentence pattern. Use these guides just like an automobile uses a specification manual. In other words, look up the parts you need to improve the structure of your sentences.

SENTENCE PATTERN 1

Subject	Verb	Direct object

Example

(subject)	(verb)	(direct object)
Mary	fixes	radios.

PARTS GUIDE FOR PATTERN 1

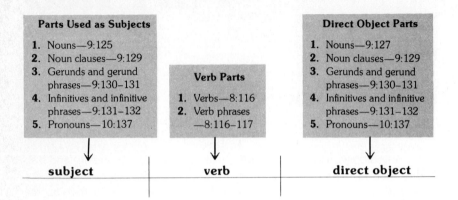

Parts Used as Subjects	Verb Parts	Direct Object Parts
1. Nouns—9:125 **2.** Noun clauses—9:129 **3.** Gerunds and gerund phrases—9:130–131 **4.** Infinitives and infinitive phrases—9:131–132 **5.** Pronouns—10:137	**1.** Verbs—8:116 **2.** Verb phrases —8:116–117	**1.** Nouns—9:127 **2.** Noun clauses—9:129 **3.** Gerunds and gerund phrases—9:130–131 **4.** Infinitives and infinitive phrases—9:131–132 **5.** Pronouns—10:137

subject   verb   direct object

Subject: A noun or noun substitute which tells what the sentence is about (see page 125).

Verb: A word or group of words which tell what the subject is doing, or which make a statement, ask a question, or give a command or direction (see page 116).

Direct object: A word or group of words which receive the action of the verb. To find a direct object, find the subject and verb, then ask a question ending with "whom" or "what."

Mary fixes what? Radios.

SENTENCE PATTERN 2

Subject	Verb	Indirect object	Direct object

Example

(subject)	(verb)	(indirect object)	(direct object)
The clerk	sold	Mac	a tire.

PARTS GUIDE FOR PATTERN 2

Note: **Refer to the guide for pattern 1 to locate parts used as subject, verb, or direct object.**

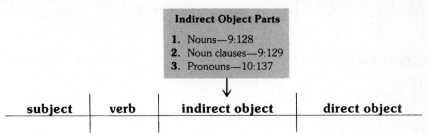

Indirect object: A word or group of words which indirectly receive the action of the verb. Most often, an indirect object answers the questions "to whom" or "for whom" something is done or given.

The clerk sold to whom? Mac.

SENTENCE PATTERN 3

Examples

(subject)	(linking verb)	(predicate adjective)
Bill	is	talented.

(subject)	(linking verb)	(predicate noun)
Nancy	is	a police officer.

PARTS GUIDE FOR PATTERN 3

Note: **Refer to guide for pattern 1 to locate parts used as subjects.**

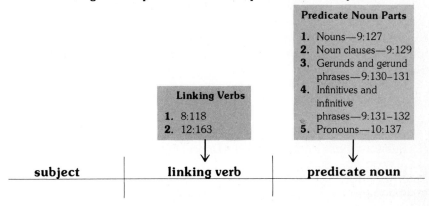

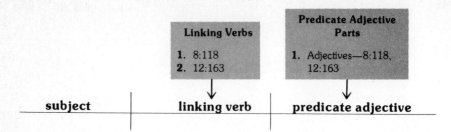

subject	linking verb	predicate adjective

Linking verb: A verb (such as *appear, be, feel, grow,* or *seem*) that connects the subject to a predicate adjective or predicate noun (see page 118).

Predicate adjective: A word or group of words which follow a linking verb and which describe the subject of the sentence (see page 118).

Predicate noun: A word or group of words which follow a linking verb and which rename the subject or stand for the same thing as the subject of the sentence (see page 118).

Look over these sentence patterns again, and pay special attention to the *parts guide.* For instance, the parts guide for the second pattern looks like this:

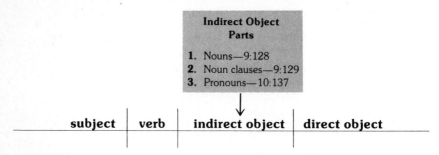

subject	verb	indirect object	direct object

From this parts list, we see that three types of words can be used as an indirect object: nouns, pronouns, and noun clauses. Each of these words is cross-referenced to specific pages in this text. Thus, if you have a question on the use of pronouns as the indirect object, this parts list refers you to page 137.

The following is a short test to see if you can easily recognize basic sentence patterns. Match the letter beside each pattern to the following sentences.

A. Subject—Verb—Direct Object

B. Subject—Verb—Indirect Object—Direct Object

C. Subject—Linking Verb—Predicate Noun

D. Subject—Linking Verb—Predicate Adjective

_____ **1.** Marty baked Ms. Jones a birthday cake.

_____ **2.** The secretary for Mr. Stone usually drinks coffee every morning at ten o'clock.

_____ **3.** The man in charge of our department was a veteran of two wars.

_____ **4.** Anthony is very intelligent.

_____ **5.** Mr. Warner gave Dad a new drill for Christmas.

_____ **6.** A capable electronics student can solve technical difficulties.

_____ **7.** The supervisor promised the workers a raise.

_____ **8.** Jan was our homecoming queen in 1976.

_____ **9.** The new physical education teacher is also a fine pianist.

_____ **10.** Mr. Barnes was not very careful when he drove the activity bus.

Answers

10.	D	5.	B
9.	C	4.	D
8.	C	3.	C
7.	B	2.	A
6.	A	1.	B

UNIT 8

Verb Problems

LEARNING OBJECTIVE

·To recognize (1) action verbs, (2) helping verbs, and (3) verb phrases

1. A verb expresses the action of the subject.

> The aircraft turned for an emergency landing.

> Martha remembered to call the switchboard supervisor.

Note: **A sentence may have two or more separate verbs.**

> The teller *smiled* and *asked* us to endorse the check.

2. In addition to action verbs, we also have helping verbs (sometimes called auxiliary verbs). Here are the twenty-three helping verbs.

was	are	has	does	should	must
were	be	had	did	would	can
is	being	have	shall	may	could
am	been	do	will	might	

Note: **Many of these helping verbs may be used alone as the main verb.**

I *had* **the wrench in my tool box.**

He *is* **strong.**

3. Whenever a main verb is combined with one, two, or three helping verbs, a verb phrase is formed.

> Apprenticeship applicants in the building trades *are required* to be in good health. (verb phrase)

> Our body shop personnel *should have repaired* the dents in your fender. (verb phrase)

The cancelled check *must have been found* by the cashier. (verb phrase)

The parts of a verb phrase may be separated by other words.

The key punch operator *did* not *transfer* the data correctly.

She *has* almost *finished* the course designed for county agricultural agents.

Parts of a verb phrase may appear first in a question.

Have you *been explaining* the final landscape design?

Has the milk *been delivered* to each store in your territory?

Note: A word ending in *-ing* or *-ed* may be used as part of a verb phrase or as an adjective.

The prisoners *were annoying* the security guards. (verb phrase)

There was an *annoying* noise in the engine. (adjective modifying noise)

Note: When you are looking for the verb in sentences containing contractions, remember that part of the contraction may represent a verb.

You*'ve ruined* the new uniforms for our employees. (*'ve* stands for have, a helping verb which is part of the verb phrase *have ruined*)

PRACTICE EXERCISE 8-A

Underline verbs and verb phrases, including all helping verbs.

1. Mary is an efficient worker.

2. I am going to enter a secretarial school next fall.

3. Have you seen our commanding officer?

4. What shall I do about that dent in my door?

5. Didn't she know about the sale?

6. When did Ray call the police officer assigned to our block?

7. Many people forget the importance of good manners.

8. The book should have been delivered last week.

9. There have never been so few candidates for the position of register of deeds.

10. Only occasionally have we had such a surprise.

LEARNING OBJECTIVE
·*To recognize linking verbs*

1. Most verbs express physical or mental action, but some verbs help to complete a statement by linking a predicate noun (a word that *stands for the same thing* as the subject) or a predicate adjective (a word that *describes* the subject) to the subject.

> *Note:* **Do not confuse the direct object with the predicate noun. The direct object will always be a word that applies to something *different* from the subject.**
>
> **Lassie is a dog. (The predicate noun** *dog* **stands for the same thing as the subject** *Lassie*. **Dog is linked to Lassie by the linking verb** *is*.**)**
>
> **Lassie is beautiful. (The predicate adjective** *beautiful* **describes the subject** *Lassie*. **The verb** *is* **links Lassie and beautiful.)**
>
> **Lassie buried a bone. (***Bone* **does not stand for Lassie; it answers the question, what did Lassie bury?** *Bone* **is the direct object, and** *buried* **is not a linking verb.)**
>
> **Notice that the verbs in the first two examples do not express action; they link the subject to the word following the verb. In the third example the verb** *buried* **tells what Lassie did.**

2. Some verbs may function as either action or linking verbs.

> Jim *looked* thin. (*looked* is a linking verb)
>
> Jim *looked* for his lab equipment. (*looked* is an action verb)
>
> Mary *appeared* in a television commercial. (action verb)
>
> Mary *appeared* happy. (linking verb)

3. The most frequently used linking verbs are the various forms of the verb *be* (is, am, are, was, were, been). Remember that forms of *be* also function as helping verbs.

> The uniforms of our drivers *are* brown. (linking verb)
>
> The wages of intercity bus drivers *are* computed on a mileage basis. (helping verb)

4. Among other words that function as linking verbs are appear, become, feel, get (when it means become), grow, remain, seem, smell, sound, and taste.

PRACTICE EXERCISE 8-B

Underline linking verbs and label predicate nouns (P.N.) and predicate adjectives (P.A.).

1. You seem too ill to complete the cost estimate by Friday.

2. William Smith became the manager of our food distribution service.

3. Our section chief will be happy.

4. Ms. Jones is the new inhalation therapist.

5. The winners of the safe-driving contest were Mary and Joe.

6. She could have been the service manager if she had applied.

7. They will be our new station attendants.

8. The cake tastes dry and our assistant chef has decided to select another recipe.

9. Mr. James Garland can be the sales manager if he completes that course in accounting.

10. The real estate representatives in the solar energy demonstration home felt comfortably warm.

LEARNING OBJECTIVE

·*To use correctly six troublesome irregular verbs*

1. lie—lay—lain
Use forms of lie when the meaning refers to a *horizontal position*.

> Please lie quietly. (present)

> Ted lay there for an hour. (past)

> The letter had lain there unopened. (past participle)

2. lay—laid—laid
Use forms of lay when the meaning is to *put down* something.

> Lay careful plans. (present)

> Jim laid the book aside. (past)

> The chicken had laid an egg. (past participle)

3. sit—sat—sat
Use forms of sit when the meaning is to *occupy a seat*.

> Tom sits there. (present)

> Marie sat near me. (past)

> You have sat there before. (past participle)

4. set—set—set

Use forms of set when the meaning is to *place something*.

> She sets the lamp on the table. (present)

> He set a good example. (past)

> You have set a good example. (past participle)

5. rise—rose—risen
Use forms of rise when the meaning is to *go up* or to *get up*.

> Will prices rise? (present)

> Father rose early this morning. (past)

> Your land has risen in value. (past participle)

6. raise—raised—raised
Use forms of raise when you mean to *lift something,* or to *make something else rise*.

> Can you raise the money? (present)

> She raised the window. (past)

> This grain was raised in Ohio. (past participle)

PRACTICE EXERCISE 8-C

Underline the correct form of the verb.

1. She spent the summer just (lying, laying) around the cottage.

2. Janice (lay, laid) the report on the president's desk and asked him to call a board meeting.

3. Bill (lay, laid) down in the back of the service truck.

4. She had (laid, lain) the paint brush on the table.

5. I saw your tools (lying, laying) on the chair.

6. She (laid, lay) her knitting aside when the salesperson called.

7. He had just (laid, lain) down when the employment agency called.

8. Extra chairs were (set, sat) in the hall for the members of the press corps.

9. James just (set, sat) there and refused to answer.

10. Mother has been (sitting, setting) by the heater all day.

11. Billie plans to (set, sit) the modular units on the hill overlooking Lake Champlain.

12. Our hopes (raised, rose) as soon as we saw the police car.

13. The river has been (rising, raising) since yesterday.

14. The neighbors helped us to (raise, rise) the trailer a few inches.

15. A cloud of dust was (rising, raising) over the tobacco field.

LEARNING OBJECTIVE
•To use the subjunctive form of a verb correctly

Read the following pairs of sentences, and try to decide whether A or B is the correct form.

A.   I wish she were here.

B.   I wish she was here.

A.   If I were you, I would not appeal the fine.

B.   If I was you, I would not report the incident.

A.   The administration building looks as if it were in need of repair.

B.   The dorm looks as if it was built ten years ago.

If you chose the answer A in all three pairs, you correctly selected the subjunctive form.

The subjunctive forms of the verb *to be* are *be* and *were*. Other verbs also have subjunctive forms, but they are far less commonly used and in most cases are the same as the present tense.

1. The subjunctive form *were* is used in statements expressing a wish.

> I wish I were going to Disney World.
>
> We wish you were here.

Note: If the wish has come true, do not use *were*.

He wished she *was* there, and she came.

2. The subjunctive form is also used in statements contrary to fact, usually after the conjunction *if* or *as if*.

> Maxine screamed as if she *were* being murdered. (Maxine is not being murdered, so this is contrary to fact.)
>
> If he *were* less boastful, he would be more popular. (He is not less boastful, so this is contrary to fact.)

Note: **When the words *would, could,* or *should* appear in the main clause of a sentence with an if clause, use the subjunctive form *were.***

3. The subjunctive form *be* is used in clauses beginning with *that* which express necessity, demand, command, or recommendation.

> She urged that the dues *be* doubled.

> We demand that our wishes *be* met.

PRACTICE EXERCISE 8-D

1. I wish I (were, was) more intelligent.

2. If you (were, are) aware of the problem, you would not be so concerned about the complaints.

3. If the supervisor (were, was) at the job site, he did not notify the contractor.

4. If his wife (were, was) at the meeting that night, she should have informed the superintendent.

5. If that (were, was) the reason for your refusal, why did you not explain it to the committee?

6. If that book (were, was) sold in California without police interference, then we will not have any difficulty with our new edition.

7. That man acts as if he (were, was) your brother.

8. If it (were, was) a nice day, we could have a picnic by the lake.

9. If she (were, was) acting sincerely, she would not be so sarcastic.

10. How wonderful this could be if it (were, was) only true.

ANSWERS TO PRACTICE EXERCISES

PRACTICE EXERCISE 8-A

1. is
2. am going
3. Have seen
4. shall do
5. Did know

6. did call
7. forget
8. should have been delivered
9. have been
10. have had

PRACTICE EXERCISE 8-B

1. *seem* ill (P.A.)

6. *could have been* manager (P.N.)

2. *became* manager (P.N.)
3. *will be* happy (P.A.)
4. *is* therapist (P.N.)
5. *were* Mary, Joe (P.N.)

7. *will be* attendants (P.N.)
8. *tastes* dry (P.A.)
9. *can be* manager (P.N.)
10. *felt* warm (P.A.)

PRACTICE EXERCISE 8-C

1. lying
2. laid
3. lay
4. laid
5. lying

6. laid
7. lain
8. set
9. sat
10. sitting

11. set
12. rose
13. rising
14. raise
15. rising

PRACTICE EXERCISE 8-D

1. were
2. were
3. was
4. were

5. was
6. was
7. were

8. were
9. were
10. were

UNIT 9

Noun Problems

LEARNING OBJECTIVE

·To recognize nouns

A noun is the name of a person, place, thing, idea, or action.

1. *Tom Jones* is a *man*.

2. *Frances* is moving to *Baltimore* soon.

3. *Women* in *art* often depict *beauty* or *justice* or *virtue*.

4. *Chickens* are hatched from *eggs*.

5. *Jogging* is good for your *health*.

PRACTICE EXERCISE 9-A

Underline all the nouns in the following sentences.

1. John is going to college

2. Phyllis enjoys the sunrise over the lake.

3. The witness agreed to tell the truth.

4. Mary and Susan live in Chicago.

5. Many animals sleep all winter.

LEARNING OBJECTIVE

•To recognize nouns used as subjects

1. The subject of a sentence is a single word or a group of words naming the person, place, thing, or idea the sentence is talking about. To find the subject first locate the verb and then ask *who?* or *what?* before *the verb.* The answer will be the subject.

> The airplane is shaped like a cigar. (The verb of this sentence is *is shaped.* By asking the question "what is shaped?" we discover that the subject of the sentence is *airplane.*

2. Quite often, a group of words may separate the subject from the verb. For example, in the sentence, *A box full of nails is on the bench, box* is the subject. *Full of nails* modifies the subject *box.*

3. In questions, the subject often separates the parts of a verb phrase.

> Has Phyllis left the circulation desk?

> To find the subject in a question, change the question into a statement; the verb phrase should emerge and you can ask, who *has left?*

> *Phyllis* has left the circulation desk.

4. Occasionally the subject does not appear in the sentence. In other words, the subject is "understood" rather than stated. For example, in sentences expressing a command or a request, the subject is always the pronoun *you,* even though the word *you* does not appear in the sentence.

> (You) Check each item on the automobile inspection form.

> (You) Please replace the oil filter and tighten the fan belt.

Note: **Remember that a subject may be compound.**

> *John* **and** *Joan* **went to the school of cosmetology.**

> *Clinics, doctors,* **and practical** *nurses* **are in short supply.**

PRACTICE EXERCISE 9-B

Underline all nouns that function as subjects in the following sentences.

1. The pharmacist works with a variety of measuring and mixing devices.

2. Jim's soldering iron was made in Germany.

3. John asks for a raise every three months.

4. Most of the errors were made during the final stages of construction.

5. Independent electrical contractors tend to locate in small towns.

6. Has Mrs. Malone finished the interview with the social worker's assistant?

7. A crate of eggs was missing from Barbara's delivery truck.

8. Mechanics and qualified technicians are in short supply.

9. Check the specification manual.

10. Rotate the tires on Saturday before noon.

LEARNING OBJECTIVE

·To distinguish between an expletive and a subject

1. The words *there* and *it* are often used as expletives and should not be confused with the subject. An expletive has no grammatical relationship to the remainder of the sentence and its only function is to get a sentence started.

> *There* was a legal *secretary* at our last meeting. (*There* is an expletive; the subject is *secretary.*)

> *It* is senseless *to apply for that position.* (*It* is an expletive; the subject is *to apply for that position.*)

Note: In most cases, it is better to reword the sentence to use an active verb rather than an expletive.

A legal secretary attended our last meeting.

Applying for that position is senseless.

2. The word *there* is never used as the subject of a sentence, but *there* may serve as an adverb at the beginning of a sentence.

> *There* is the *place* to put it. (*There* is an adverb.)

3. The word *it* may also be used as the pronoun subject of a sentence (see page 137).

> *It* is in the cabinet. (*It* is the subject.)

PRACTICE EXERCISE 9-C

Write *expl.* above any word used as an expletive. Rewrite each sentence that contains an expletive in such a manner that the expletive is removed.

1. There is the sander under your workbench.

2. It is over there next to the furnace.

3. It is useless to apply the rules to this case.

4. There are six towns in our school district.

5. There was a huge rock in the road.

6. It is a large factory.

7. There is always a correct way.

8. There he goes.

9. It seems to me that you have done a good job.

10. It is a beautiful sunset.

LEARNING OBJECTIVE

·To label correctly nouns used as direct objects or as predicate nouns

1. The direct object directly receives the action of the verb or shows the result of the action. Locating the direct object is easy if we first say the subject and the verb, and then ask *what?* or *whom?* Our answer to these questions (what? or whom?) will be the direct object.

> The meteorologist predicted a hurricane. (The meteorologist predicted what? Answer: hurricane—D.O.)

> Wind destroyed the trailer. (Wind destroyed what? Answer: trailer—D.O.)

2. A direct object may be compound.

> We remember Elizabeth and Joan very well. (We remember whom? Answer: Elizabeth, Joan—D.O.'s)

3. Do not confuse the direct object with a predicate noun. Remember that a predicate noun is a word which *stands for the same thing as the subject.* Also, the predicate noun is used with a linking verb.

> Betty is the health inspector. (P.N.)

> Ernie cleaned his baking ovens. (D.O.)

Note: **The direct objects and predicate nouns usually follow the verb, but for special effect they may be placed before the verb.**

> **This** *job* **I really enjoyed. (D.O.)**

> **Our** *leader* **he isn't. (P.N.)**

Write D.O. above direct objects and P.N. above predicate nouns.

1. Medical record librarians prepare reports on patients' illnesses and treatments.

2. In some hospitals practical nurses receive pay increases after specified periods of satisfactory service.

3. Joyce was our babysitter for one year before she entered nurses' training.

4. Many hospitals provide free meals and uniforms.

5. Our new truck mechanic is Mr. Jones.

6. She expected a better grade on her fitness report.

7. That newspaper provides the best information on employment opportunities.

8. Potential salespersons often measure their abilities through summer vacation sales positions.

9. Successful insurance agents have persuasive personalities.

10. Ralph is the head nurse on the third floor.

LEARNING OBJECTIVE
•To label correctly nouns used as indirect objects

1. The indirect object shows *to whom* or *for whom* the action is done. The indirect object is usually found between the verb and the direct object.

> Father made David a boat. (Father made what? Answer: boat—D.O. For whom did father make the boat? Answer: David—I.O.)

2. An indirect object may be compound.

> Mother gave Steven and Ben advice about their vocational interests. (To whom did mother give advice? Answer: Steven, Ben—I.O.'s)

PRACTICE EXERCISE 9-E

Write I.O. above indirect objects and D.O. above direct objects.

1. Mr. Green gave Robert a new drafting pencil.

2. The committee sent Mrs. Nader an estimate of the building costs.

3. Craig bought Jamie a new kiln for her pottery classes.

4. Carl gave Nell the blueprint for her new garage.

5. Rosa sent Louise and Audry an invitation to the office party.

LEARNING OBJECTIVE

•To recognize noun clauses, and how they function in a sentence

1. Basically, there are two types of clauses: main (or independent) and dependent (or subordinate). Both types have a subject and a verb. The main clause expresses a complete thought and can stand alone as a sentence. The dependent clause *does not express a complete thought* and *is always attached to a main clause.*

> John wanted a new car. (main clause)
>
> She is in my class. (main clause)
>
> what John wanted (dependent clause)
>
> who she is (dependent clause)

2. A noun clause is a group of words which has a subject and a verb and functions in the same way as a one-word noun.

> *Where I decide to live* will be determined by my job. (noun clause as subject)
>
> This small battery is *what the transmitter needs.* (noun clause as a predicate noun)
>
> I believe *that Mr. Wilson spoke about the new wiring code.* (noun clause as direct object)

Note: The word *that* **is often omitted or "understood" when it introduces a noun clause functioning as a direct object.**

> **I believe** *(that) Mr. Wilson spoke about the new wiring code.*

> We were fascinated by *what the teacher said.* (noun clause as object of a preposition)
>
> Give *whoever calls* the message about registration. (noun clause as indirect object)

Note: The words *that, what, whatever, how, why, whether, if, when, where, whose, who, whoever, which,* **and** *whichever* **often introduce noun clauses and connect them to the sentence.**

PRACTICE EXERCISE 9-F

Underline each noun clause and write its function above the clause.

1. How this business decision was made has not been explained to our attorney.

2. Whether we go to the conference depends on how we perform on the job.

3. I wonder where the lawyer's assistant received his special training.

4. A fresh approach is what I need for my paper on environmental health.

5. She has no idea of what is involved in replacing a shock absorber.

6. That we gave the pipefitters another chance proved to be the best solution to our plumbing problems.

7. Mr. Thomas offered whoever fixes his limousine a fifty dollar bonus.

8. That a strike was avoided is most encouraging.

9. Has the police department determined whose car was used?

10. The trouble is they were not aware of the importance of mechanical aptitude.

LEARNING OBJECTIVE
·To recognize gerunds used as nouns

1. We can turn any verb into a gerund by adding *ing* to it. (Sometimes a minor change in spelling is also needed.) However, remember that the verb plus *ing* is not a gerund *unless it functions as a noun.* Compare the following examples:

   > We *were painting* the ceiling. (verb; in this example *"painting"* is part of a verb phrase.)

   > *Painting* is my favorite hobby. (gerund; in this example *"painting"* is the subject of the sentence and thus has a noun function)

2. Gerunds function in most of the ways that nouns function.

   > *Banking* often involves complicated financial transactions. (subject)

   > I enjoy *baking.* (D.O.)

   > An enjoyable pastime is *reading.* (P.N.)

3. Other words may be added to gerunds to form gerund phrases.

Voting in a booth has become standard. (gerund phrase as subject)

John admitted *going to the ball game instead of school.* (gerund phrase as direct object)

An excellent business is *selling electrical appliances.* (gerund phrase as predicate noun)

Note: Gerund phrases also function as noun appositives; refer to Unit 13 (page 181) for an example of a gerund phrase appositive which requires commas. Unit 13 also includes an example of a gerund phrase object of a preposition which occurs in a position where it requires a comma (see page 177).

PRACTICE EXERCISE 9-G

Underline each gerund phrase, and write its function as a noun above each phrase (subject, direct object, predicate noun).

1. Mother has always enjoyed working as a dietitian in the county hospital.

2. Planning a career in banking involves a careful assessment of one's ability to work with figures.

3. The manager's main job is developing new methods of servicing business machines.

4. An interesting pastime is building a radio from spare parts.

5. Patsy enjoys serving gourmet meals on the evening flight to Los Angeles.

6. Taking a raincoat to the game was an excellent idea.

7. Dad enjoys refinishing antique tables.

8. The agent's job is finding stolen goods.

9. Washing clothes takes too much of Jean's time.

10. The President's chief interest is winning re-election.

LEARNING OBJECTIVE
•To recognize infinitives as nouns

1. An infinitive is made of *to* plus a verb, and may be used as a noun.

   To build is our hope. (infinitive as subject)

   Mary hopes *to pass.* (infinitive as direct object)

My ambition is *to graduate.* (infinitive as predicate noun)

He wants nothing except *to succeed.* (infinitive as object of a preposition; see page 168)

2. Other words may be added to infinitives to form infinitive phrases.

To obtain a high school diploma is important for anyone interested in entering the business world. (infinitive phrase as subject)

My company hopes *to use plastics in building construction.* (infinitive phrase as direct object)

The cement mason's job is *to lay a mastic coating over concrete.* (infinitive phrase as predicate noun)

Jane wants nothing but *to help her drafting students.* (infinitive phrase as object of a preposition; see page 168)

3. Do not confuse the infinitive with a prepositional phrase that begins with *to.*

Note: **A preposition is a word that shows the relation of a noun or pronoun (called its object) to some other word in the sentence. A prepositional phrase is made up of a preposition, its object, and any words that modify its object.**

Compare the following examples.

infinitives	**prepositional phrases**
to store	(go) to the store
to play	(go) to a play

You will be able to tell these apart more easily if you remember that the second part of an infinitive is always a verb, and the object of a preposition is always a noun or pronoun.

4. Sometimes the *to* of an infinitive is omitted (or understood).

Al helped his father (to) trim the hedge.

Note: **Infinitives and infinitive phrases also function as adjectives and as adverbs. Only rarely, however, does this use of infinitives cause writing problems or require punctuation. However, when an infinitive phrase serves as an appositive, commas must be used, and in the comma unit there is an example of an infinitive phrase requiring a comma when it functions as an adverb modifying the verb in the main part of the sentence (see comma unit, page 177).**

PRACTICE EXERCISE 9-H

Underline infinitive phrases, and above each phrase write its function as a noun.

1. To develop an economical source of energy has been our primary goal for the past three years.

2. Every carpenter's ambition is to be accepted as a highly skilled worker.

3. Our line mechanics hope to complete the landing gear inspection before six o'clock.

4. Dick's principal goal is to qualify for on-the-job training as a radiation monitor.

5. We have done everything except request the services of a landscape architect.

6. His job is to set the timing.

7. Her chief aim is to succeed in college.

8. Martha wants nothing but to help her students.

9. I hope to earn twenty dollars in tips.

10. Everyone desires to be trusted.

ANSWERS TO PRACTICE EXERCISES

PRACTICE EXERCISE 9-A

1. *John, college*
2. *Phyllis, sunrise, lake*
3. *witness, truth*
4. *Mary, Susan, Chicago*
5. *animals, winter*

PRACTICE EXERCISE 9-B

1. *pharmacist*
2. *iron*
3. *John*
4. (The subject in this sentence is *Most*, a pronoun)
5. *contractors*
6. *Mrs. Malone*
7. *crate*
8. *mechanics, technicians*
9. [In this sentence the subject is *You* (understood)]
10. *You* (understood) is the subject

PRACTICE EXERCISE 9-C

1. No expletive
2. No expletive
3. It (expl.); Applying the rules to this case is useless.

4. There (expl.); Six towns belong to our school district.
5. There (expl.); A huge rock lay in the road.
6. No expletive
7. There (expl.); A correct way always exists.
8. No expletive
9. It (expl.); I think you have done a good job.
10. No expletive

PRACTICE EXERCISE 9-D

1. reports (D.O.)
2. increases (D.O.)
3. babysitter (P.N.)
4. meals, uniforms (D.O.'s)
5. Mr. Jones (P.N.)
6. grade (D.O.)
7. information (D.O.)
8. abilities (D.O.)
9. personalities (D.O.)
10. nurse (P.N.)

PRACTICE EXERCISE 9-E

1. Robert (I.O.), pencil (D.O.)
2. Mrs. Nader (I.O.), estimate (D.O.)
3. Jamie (I.O.), kiln (D.O.)
4. Nell (I.O.), blueprint (D.O.)
5. Louise, Audry (I.O.'s), invitation (D.O.)

PRACTICE EXERCISE 9-F

1. *How this business decision was made* (subject)
2. *Whether we go to the conference* (subject)
   how we perform on the job (object of a preposition)
3. *where the lawyer's assistant received his special training* (direct object)
4. *what I need for my paper on environmental health* (predicate noun)
5. *what is involved in replacing a shock absorber* (object of a preposition)
6. *That we give the pipefitters another chance* (subject)
7. *whoever fixes his limousine* (indirect object)
8. *That a strike was avoided* (subject)
9. *whose car was used* (direct object)
10. *[that] they were not aware of the importance of mechanical aptitude* (predicate noun)

PRACTICE EXERCISE 9-G

1. *working as a dietitian in the county hospital* (direct object)
2. *Planning a career in banking* (subject)
3. *developing new methods of servicing business machines* (predicate noun)
4. *building a radio from spare parts* (predicate noun)
5. *serving gourmet meals on the evening flight to Los Angeles* (direct object)
6. *Taking a raincoat to the game* (subject)
7. *refinishing antique tables* (direct object)
8. *finding stolen goods* (predicate noun)

9. *Washing clothes* (subject)
10. *winning re-election* (predicate noun)

PRACTICE EXERCISE 9-H

1. *To develop an economical source of energy* (subject)
2. *to be accepted as a highly skilled worker* (predicate noun)
3. *to complete the landing gear inspection before six o'clock* (direct object)
4. *to qualify for on-the-job training as a radiation monitor* (predicate noun)
5. *(to) request the services of a landscape architect* (object of a preposition)
6. *to set the timing* (predicate noun)
7. *to succeed in college* (predicate noun)
8. *to help her students* (object of a preposition)
9. *to earn twenty dollars in tips* (direct object)
10. *to be trusted* (predicate noun)

UNIT 10

Pronoun Problems

A pronoun is a word used in place of a noun. For example, *he, she,* and *it* are pronouns. If you understand the basic function of nouns, it should not be difficult to use pronouns correctly.

Suppose you were told *to remove the picture tube from the television set and throw it away.* In this situation the pronoun *it* does not clearly refer to either the picture tube or the television set. You could easily have thrown away a perfectly good TV when it was actually the picture tube that your supervisor wanted you to discard. You see that errors in *pronoun reference* can cause serious misunderstandings.

Errors in *pronoun agreement* can also cause confusion. If you say that *John and Jim left the factory with his new tools,* it is not clear who owns the tools. The pronoun *his* could refer to either John or Jim, or to a third person. Pronouns must agree in number with the word(s) they apply to. In this case, if both John and Jim have new tools, we say *their* new tools. If only one has new tools, you must reword the sentence; for example, *John left the factory with Jim, who took along his new tools.* Clearly, many occupational situations require the correct use of pronouns.

LEARNING OBJECTIVE

•*To use the correct form of a personal pronoun and to recognize its function within a sentence*

1. There are three forms of personal pronouns: the nominative form, the objective form, and the possessive form. *Use the nominative form when the personal pronoun is the subject of a sentence or is a predicate noun; use the objective form when the personal pronoun is a direct object, an indirect object, or the object of a preposition. Use the possessive form to*

show possession. The first possessive form is used when the pronoun precedes the noun it modifies (her car); the second when it stands alone (it is hers). (See Unit 14, page 205, for use of possessives.)

Nominative form	Objective form	Possessive form	
I	me	my, mine	
you	you	your, yours	
he	him	his	Singular
she	her	her, hers	
it	it	its	
we	us	our, ours	
you	you	your, yours	Plural
they	them	their, theirs	

2. The *nominative form* of personal pronouns is used as the subject of a sentence or as a predicate noun.

> *They* were in the ornamental iron business for years. (subject)

> It was *she*. (predicate noun)

3. The *objective form* of pronouns is used as direct object, indirect object, or object of a preposition.

> The shipping clerk called *her*. (direct object)

> He called *them*. (direct object)

> The manager gave *him* some advice about finishing plates for color printing. (indirect object)

> The press operators gave *her* a unique metal container. (indirect object)

> The secretaries caught a ride with *him*. (object of a preposition)

> Wait for *me* to finish repairing the phototypesetting machine. (object of a preposition)

4. Most pronoun errors occur in compound constructions. The following exercises will not be difficult *if you can decide how the pronoun is used in the sentence*. Here is a simple formula to keep in mind; *I, he, she, we, they* should be used as a subject or predicate noun; *me, him, her, us, them* should be used as a direct object, indirect object, or object of a preposition. As you apply the formula, it is helpful to analyze each half of a compound construction separately.

> Bill and (I, me) are training to be industrial machinery repairpersons. (In analyzing this sentence you can see that *Bill* is half of the compound subject. The formula tells you that *me* cannot function as the

subject, and it then becomes clear that the correct pronoun in this example is *I*.)

Note: **Do not be confused by an appositive that immediately follows a pronoun (we women, us men, we seniors). Analyze sentences that include these combinations by** *omitting the appositive and applying the preceding formula.*

PRACTICE EXERCISE 10-A

Underline the correct pronoun form inside each parenthesis. Above your answer write the function of the pronoun you select. Use the following abbreviations: Subj., D.O., O.P., I.O., P.N.

1. Kathy and (me, I) qualified for flight engineers' certificates.

2. It was (they, them).

3. The company policy regarding absenteeism was written by Ms. Jackson and (she, her).

4. The state patrol officer visited Tommy and (he, him).

5. (We, Us) men will help the custodian clean out the basement.

6. Did you leave the meter reader and (she, her) in the service van?

7. Mr. Stone will give you and (her, she) another chance to complete the calibration of the chemical analysis instruments.

8. The ranger protects (we, us) visitors from danger.

9. Ruth and (her, she) are trying to coordinate the quality control department.

10. Neither Ed nor (they, them) can complete the dental hygienist course until next summer.

11. (We, Us) men will be seasonal rangers.

12. (They, Them) and their assistants protect life and property.

13. Are (us, we) women invited to the science fair?

14. A dispute arose between their scout leader and (they, them).

15. Show Carol and (me, I) the new wire-wrapping tool used by the central office installers.

16. Working in the film editing department usually relaxes Doyle and (I, me).

17. I shall take Janet and (she, her) to observe the power tool demonstration.

18. Either Jack or (her, she) will write to you regarding the earnings of boilermakers.

19. Give the message to either Betty or (her, she).

20. When are you and (she, her) going to apply for the offset printing position?

LEARNING OBJECTIVE

•*To use correctly the pronouns* who *and* whom, *according to their function in the sentence*

1. *Who* is the nominative form and is used as a subject or a predicate noun.

> *Who* came first? (subject)

> The leader is *who*? (predicate noun)

> *Note:* **Whoever** *is also the nominative form and functions in the same way* who *functions.*

2. *Whom* is the objective form and is used as a direct object, indirect object, or object of a preposition.

> *Whom* do you want? (direct object)

> He gave *whom* the diagram? (indirect object)

> To *whom* did you give the keys to the wrecker? (object of a preposition)

> *Hint:* **Whom** *usually follows a preposition.*

> *Note:* **Whomever** *is the objective form and functions in the same way* whom *functions.*

3. When *who (whoever)* and *whom (whomever)* are used to begin a dependent clause, their form is determined by their use in the clause. The form is not affected by any word outside the clause. Follow three simple steps as you analyze a who-whom problem at the beginning of a dependent clause. First, isolate the clause.
Second, decide how *who (whoever)* or *whom (whomever)* functions within the clause.
Third, apply the following formula:

> *Who (whoever)* functions only as the subject or the predicate noun of a clause.

Whom (whomever) functions only as the direct object, indirect object, or object of a preposition.

The new load dispatcher, *(who, whom) has taken Mr. Smith's position,* is from a small town in the West. (First, underline the clause. Second, notice that *has taken* is the verb of the clause and that the subject of the clause is either *who* or *whom*. Third, apply the formula: only *who* can be the subject.)

The senior broadcasting technician, *(who, whom) I met yesterday, monitors and logs outgoing signals and is responsible for proper operation of the transmitter. (I* is the subject of the clause and *met* is the verb. The direct object of *met* is *whom.)*

Give the plans to *(whomever, whoever) calls.* (At first glance it would appear that the correct answer would be *whomever* because you usually think of the word *whom* as correctly following the preposition *to.* However, when you isolate and analyze the underlined clause, you realize that whoever is the correct answer because only *whoever* can serve as the subject of the clause.)

Note: **In determining the use of** *who* **or** *whom,* **do not be misled by a parenthetical expression such as** *I think, do you think,* **or** *he said.* **Simply cover up these expressions and analyze the remainder of the sentence according to the procedure outlined above.**

She is a person *who* **(, I believe,)** *should be promoted.* **(A parenthetical expression of this type does not affect the clause.)**

PRACTICE EXERCISE 10-B

Underline either *who* or *whom*. Write the function of your answers above the parentheses. Use the following abbreviations to indicate function: Subj., P.N., D.O., I.O., O.P.

1. (Who, Whom) came first?

2. The paper machine operator is (whom, who)?

3. To (who, whom) did you give the data on wages in pulp plants?

4. He gave (whom, who) the inventory records?

5. The payroll clerk is (who, whom)?

6. For (whom, who) are you inspecting those cartons?

7. (Who, Whom) shall I send to regulate the flow of pulp onto the papermaking machine?

8. (Whom, Who) do you think will operate the chipper machine in our paper mill?

9. Everybody (who, whom) received an invitation will attend the company picnic.

10. The teachers (who, whom) are on strike would prefer to be at school.

11. The assembly-line workers (whom, who) I most admire are the seat trimmers and the platers who apply chrome to bumpers.

12. If we had known (who, whom) he was, he would have explained the assembly-line process more carefully.

13. The union officers will be (whoever, whomever) the committee nominates.

14. Since she did not know (whom, who) the memo was for, she decided not to open it.

15. Send the job application to (whomever, whoever) writes first.

LEARNING OBJECTIVE
·To have a pronoun agree in number *with its antecedent*

1. The antecedent of a pronoun is the word or words the pronoun stands for. Agreement in number is achieved when a *singular* pronoun refers to a *singular* antecedent, and when a *plural* pronoun refers to a *plural* antecedent.

> *Neither* of the concrete finishers was exempted from *his* apprenticeship requirements.

> The cement *masons* in our company submitted *their* request for a raise.

2. Singular pronouns (he, him, his, she, her, hers, it, its) are used to refer to the following words: either, neither, each, one, no one, everyone, anyone, someone, everybody, nobody, anybody, and somebody. A phrase immediately following these words does not change their number.

> *Each* of the floor covering installers had removed *her* shoes.

> *No one* in the office had given *his* permission to extend the coffee hour past eleven o'clock.

Note: When an antecedent may be either masculine or feminine, a masculine pronoun (he, him, his) is commonly used to refer to the antecedent. Although some people find this offensive, no generally accepted substitute has yet been found.

> If *anyone* **drives to the construction site this afternoon, ask** *him* **to pick up the wallboard and plywood stacked beside the architect's trailer.**

3. Two or more antecedents joined by *and* are referred to by a plural pronoun.

> *Mary* and *Rita* left the commissary with their new security guard uniforms.

4. Two or more singular antecedents joined by *or* or *nor* are referred to by a singular pronoun.

> Neither *Jerry* nor *Jack* was responsible for *his* failure to complete the automobile inspection form.

> (Exception) Neither *Jerry* nor *Betty* was responsible for *their* failure to stop at the factory entrance.

Note: **In cases like the exception shown here, it is often clearer if you reword the sentence.**

> **Neither Jerry nor Betty was responsible for failing to stop at the factory entrance.**

Caution: **When one of the two antecedents joined by** *or* **or** *nor* **is singular and one is plural, the pronoun usually agrees with the nearer.**

> **Neither Mr. Lee nor his** *employees* **were certain of** *their* **roles in the evacuation plan.**

PRACTICE EXERCISE 10-C

Underline the pronouns in parentheses that agree with their antecedents.

1. Mack and Joan were asked to describe (their, his, her) window display.

2. Everybody who submits a job application knows that (he, they) will have to drive carefully to qualify for the rural mail carrier position.

3. Either Wayne or John will be asked to make (their, his) computer printout results available to all employees.

4. Neither of the girls was blamed for (her, their) part in the chemical laboratory accident.

5. Each of the bookkeeping machine operators was asked to report (her, his) findings.

6. Neither Alfredo nor his brothers were required to report (his, their) traffic violations to the social worker.

7. If someone decides to drive the bus to our picnic, please ask (them, her, him) to sign out before the garage mechanics leave.

8. Neither Alton nor Stuart was asked to repeat (his, their) medical laboratory analysis.

9. After the assistant superintendent had persuaded somebody to drive, (they, he) refused to accept the responsibility for the safety of the passengers.

10. Either one of the men may ride (his, their) motorcycle to the assembly plant.

LEARNING OBJECTIVE
•To have pronouns refer clearly to their antecedents

1. The antecedent of a pronoun is the word or idea to which a pronoun refers.

> We invited *Allen* but *he* could not attend the sales meeting. (In this sentence the pronoun *he* refers to the noun *Allen; Allen* is the antecedent of *he*.)

2. A pronoun must refer clearly to its antecedent. For correct reference, place a pronoun as close as possible to its antecedent.

> The union organizer was liked by everyone who managed to get along well with people. (unclear)

> The union organizer, who managed to get along well with people, was liked by everyone. (better)

3. If close placement does not achieve clear reference, you should repeat the antecedent, use a synonym for the antecedent, or rewrite the entire sentence.

> Mary brought a glove, and Jack carried the softball. They were both old and wrinkled. (unclear)

> Mary brought a glove, and Jack carried the softball. Both glove and ball were old and wrinkled. (better)

4. Avoid ambiguous reference. Ambiguous reference occurs when a pronoun stands in place of more than one antecedent, which gives the sentence more than one possible meaning.

> Remove the *motor* from your *tractor* and sell it. (Do you sell the *motor* or the *tractor*?)

Rewrite the sentence to avoid ambiguity.

Sell the motor after you remove it from your tractor.

Occasionally it may be necessary to remove the pronoun and repeat the noun it refers to or to quote the exact words of the speaker.

(ambiguous) Jim told Bob that he was too young to join the union.

(clear) Jim told Bob that Bob was too young to join the union.

(clear) Jim said to Bob, "You are too young to join the union."

5. Avoid general pronoun references. Pronouns that refer to general ideas in a preceding sentence or to unspecified ideas of any kind may not be clear to the reader.

The employees in our department were assessed ten dollars for leaving the shop cluttered with litter. *This* caused their superintendent to change the company's regulations. (What is the pronoun *this* referring to? the assessment or the litter?)

(correction) The ten dollar assessment of the employees caused their superintendent to change the company's regulations.

The janitor cleaned the entrance to the gym, which the principal approved of. (The pronoun *which* appears to refer to gym, but the reader cannot be certain. *Which* could refer to *entrance*.)

(correction) The principal approved of the manner in which the janitor had cleaned the entrance to the gym.

6. Avoid weak pronoun reference. Weak reference occurs when the antecedent exists only in the writer's mind.

James wrote in his spare time, but none of it was ever published. (The pronoun *it* should refer to the gerund noun *writing*, but *writing* does not appear in the sentence).

7. Avoid referring to an antecedent in the possessive case.

After Frazier's workers completed the paving project, he allowed them to take an extra day off.

(improved) Mr. Frazier allowed his workers to take an extra day off after they completed the paving project.

8. Avoid the awkward and indefinite use of the pronouns *it, you,* and *they.*

If employees do not observe the employee dress code *you* may be fired.

(improved) If employees do not observe the dress code *they* may be fired.

On ships that cross oceans *they* provide a doctor without charge.

(improved) On ships that cross oceans a doctor is provided at no extra charge.

In the final unit *it* says that memos are not difficult to write.

(improved) The final unit says that memos are not difficult to write.

PRACTICE EXERCISE 10-D

Correct errors in pronoun reference by rewriting the following sentences.

1. Betty told Alice that she could take the course in diesel mechanics.

_____

_____

2. Remove the compressor from the refrigerator and throw it away.

_____

_____

3. Michelle was working with Grace and she seemed very happy.

_____

_____

4. She is an intelligent, hard-working young person with an exciting personality, but it doesn't make her any happier.

_____

_____

_____

5. Due to illness Marvin was unable to work during the most important phase of the bridge construction, which caused much unhappiness among the other builders.

_____

_____

_____

6. I appreciated their customer service record and the attitude of their employees. It made me want to write a commendation letter to the general manager.

_____

_____

_____

7. Mrs. Canfield has invested heavily in the automotive industry, but despite the recent rise in prices she never sells any of it.

_____

_____

_____

8. Before Ms. Martin's sales personnel boarded the bus, she told them she was pleased at their ability to convince the buyers to accept a new product.

_____

_____

_____

9. In the service manual it says that a knowledge of electronics is necessary to perform some appliance repair jobs.

_____

_____

_____

10. During a baseball game with Central, Lee threw the bat about ten feet after hitting a home run, made faces at the umpire, and shouted obscenities at the opposing team. This annoyed Coach Drake.

_____

_____

_____

LEARNING OBJECTIVE
•To solve special pronoun problems

1. As a general rule, use the possessive form immediately before a gerund.

Her leaving the office before five o'clock became a problem.

Mr. Brooks approved of *(my, his, her, our, your, their)* taking a fifteen-minute coffee break.

2. The form for pronouns following *than* or *as* is more easily determined if you supply words that are understood and not written in.

She is stronger than *I* (am). (In this example the reader chooses the pronoun *I* rather than *me* because only *I* can be the subject of the unwritten verb *am.*)

James is as rich as *they* (are).

Mrs. Bell is older than *I* (am).

3. If the pronoun is the object of a verb that is understood, use the objective form.

The supervisor needs him more than (he needs) *me.*

I defeated him as well as (I defeated) *her.*

4. Use the nominative form after the verb *be.*

It was (I, he, she, we, or they).

Note: **Informal use accepts** *It is me* **and** *It's me* **instead of** *It's I,* **which sounds awkward to many people.**

PRACTICE EXERCISE 10-E

Underline the correct pronoun form within the parentheses.

1. June is as young as (her, she).

2. The principal approves of (you, your) going to a technical institute.

3. Janice is more mature than (I, me).

4. We are proud of (him, his, her) taking the course in automobile mechanics.

5. Did you know about (me, my) playing a solo at the band concert?

ANSWERS TO PRACTICE EXERCISES

PRACTICE EXERCISE 10-A

1. I (subj.)	8. us (d.o.)	15. me (i.o.)
2. they (p.n.)	9. she (subj.)	16. me (d.o.)
3. her (o.p.)	10. they (subj.)	17. her (d.o.)
4. him (d.o.)	11. We (subj.)	18. she (subj.)
5. We (subj.)	12. They (subj.)	19. her (o.p.)
6. her (d.o.)	13. we (subj.)	20. she (subj.)
7. her (i.o.)	14. them (o.p.)	

PRACTICE EXERCISE 10-B

1. Who (subj.)
2. who (p.n.)
3. whom (o.p.)
4. whom (i.o.)
5. who (p.n.)
6. whom (o.p.)
7. Whom (d.o.)
8. Who (subj.)
9. who (subj.)
10. who (subj.)
11. whom (d.o.)
12. who (p.n.)
13. whomever (d.o.)
14. whom (o.p.)
15. whoever (subj.)

PRACTICE EXERCISE 10-C

1. their
2. he
3. his
4. her
5. his
6. their
7. him
8. his
9. he
10. his

PRACTICE EXERCISE 10-D

1. Betty said to Alice, "You may take the course in diesel mechanics."
2. Throw the compressor away after you remove it from the refrigerator.
3. When she was working with Grace, Michelle seemed very happy.
4. She is an intelligent, hard-working young person with an exciting personality, but these qualities do not make her any happier.
5. Marvin's inability to work during the most important phase of the bridge construction caused much unhappiness among the other builders.
6. I appreciated their customer service record and their employees' attitude; such concern for their customers made me want to write a commendation letter to the general manager.
7. Mrs. Canfield has invested heavily in the auto industry, but despite the recent rise in prices she never sells any of her automotive stocks.
8. Before her sales personnel boarded the bus, Ms. Martin told them she was pleased at their ability to convince the buyers to accept a new product.
9. The service manual says that a knowledge of electronics is necessary to perform some appliance repair jobs.
10. During a baseball game with Central, Lee annoyed Coach Drake by throwing the bat about ten feet after hitting a home run, by making faces at the umpire, and by shouting obscenities at the opposing team.

PRACTICE EXERCISE 10-E

1. she
2. your
3. I
4. his, her
5. my

UNIT 11

Subject-Verb Agreement

By learning how subjects and verbs agree, you can avoid the negative impression that would result if you applied for a job and said, "I types sixty words a minute," or "We has two children." Each of these statements is an example of a verb that does not agree with its subject.

LEARNING OBJECTIVE
•To locate the subject of a sentence

The first step in solving subject-verb agreement problems is to locate the subject of the sentence. You will recall from Unit 8 that you first find the verb and then ask who? or what? before the verb. Your answer will be the subject.

> One of the cylinders was missing in the used car. (In this sentence the verb is *was missing*. When you answer the question what was missing? you realize that the subject is *one*.)

Three kinds of sentence construction often make it difficult to locate the subject.

1. A prepositional phrase following a singular subject may easily confuse you, especially if the phrase includes a noun that appears to be the subject.

> The *timing* of those engines *was adjusted* by our most experienced mechanic. (In this example notice that the prepositional phrase *of those engines* separates the subject, *timing*, from the verb, *was adjusted*. Do not make the mistake of thinking that *engines* is the subject.)

2. Interrupting phrases introduced by such words as *besides, along with, like, with, no less than, as well as, together with, in addition to,* or *including* may also contain a word or words you could mistakenly identify as the subject.

> *Maxine* and *Jenny,* like Mrs. Johnson, *were* late for the sales orienta-

tion. (In this example notice that Mrs. Johnson is part of the interrupting phrase, which you should ignore when locating the subject of the sentence.)

3. In sentences that begin with *here is, here are, there is, there are, where is,* and *where are,* the subject follows the verb.

Where are your *brother* and *sister?* The subject is *brother* and *sister.*)

PRACTICE EXERCISE 11-A

Underline the subject once and the verb twice in the sentences below.

1. There are many possible candidates at the conference.

2. The forest ranger, as well as a large number of the animals in his district, was in danger of being trapped by the fire sweeping the north ridge.

3. Mr. Berry, together with his two sons, has been primarily responsible for operating our drilling rig in the Gulf of Mexico.

4. The decision of the patrol officers was final.

5. Here are the nails you ordered.

6. The signs at the top of the building were not lighted.

7. Everything but the tools was in the back of the truck.

8. His objections to our program seem unimportant.

9. The ship, with its entire crew and cargo, was lost at sea.

10. The faculty, as well as the principal, was enthusiastic about the new vocational education program.

LEARNING OBJECTIVE

·To determine the number of the subject

Failing to have the subject of a sentence agree in number with the verb is one of the most common problems in both written and spoken English. In grammar, the term *number* refers to the *number of units* you are talking about. English has only two numbers: singular (one unit) and plural (more than one unit).

You already know that nouns and pronouns may be used as subjects. It is important to know that nouns and pronouns also have number. In the brief lists below you will see how number is involved.

Nouns referring to one unit (singular):	Nouns referring to more than one unit (plural):
hammer	books
ball	tools
telephone	tires

The *ball* is on the table. (one unit)

The *tires* are new. (more than one unit)

Pronouns referring to one unit (singular):	Pronouns referring to more than one unit (plural):
I, he, she, it, this, that	we, they, these, those

That is mine. (one unit)

Those are yours. (more than one unit)

You will probably have little trouble determining the number of words like *book* or *books*. However, a number of sentence constructions and nouns are troublesome. The following list describes some of these.

1. Compound subjects joined by *and* are usually plural.

> *Martha* and *Meg* are good friends. (plural)

Note: **Sometimes a compound subject is considered as one unit (singular).**

> *Ham and eggs* **is my favorite breakfast dish. (singular; ham and eggs is one dish)**

Note: **When the words *every* and *many a* are followed by a word or series of words, the subject is considered to be a singular unit.**

> *Every* **bat, ball, and glove in the sports show** *was* **expertly displayed by our department manager. (singular)**

> *Many a* **counselor** *has refused* **to divulge information about a client's personal life. (singular)**

2. When two singular subjects are joined by *or, nor, either . . . or,* and *neither . . . nor,* only one unit (singular) is being referred to.

> A *doctor* or a medical *specialist* is standing by. (singular; only one is standing by)

3. A collective noun is plural when the speaker is thinking of the individual members of the group. (*Note:* A collective noun is one that has a singular form but refers to a group of people or things.)

> The *family* have agreed among themselves to go to the beach. (plural; the individual members have agreed)

Our *crew* have been discussing the plans for a new building site. (plural; the individuals making up the crew have been discussing the plans)

A collective noun is singular when the group is considered as one unit.

The *family* is going on a picnic. (singular; one family unit)

4. Some nouns are plural in form but have a singular meaning and are therefore considered as one unit.

mathematics (is, not are)	genetics (is)	mumps (is)
measles (is)	physics (is)	semantics (is)
civics (is)	news (is)	linguistics (is)
economics (is)		

Caution: Some nouns that end in *-ics* are singular when they refer to an organized body of knowledge and plural when they refer to separate facts.

Statistics is a difficult subject. (singular)

The statistics were difficult to understand. (plural)

Acoustics is an interesting subject. (singular)

The acoustics in our church are excellent. (plural)

5. The words *the number* refer to one unit (singular).

The number of employees is increasing. (singular; one quantity of employees)

The words *a number* have a plural meaning and function.

A number of children have been vaccinated. (plural)

6. Fractions denoting a fixed quantity or amount (two-thirds, five percent) are considered as one unit (singular).

Ten percent of the land is under water. (singular; one portion of land)

When a fraction is followed by a phrase that contains a plural word, the fraction is a plural noun.

Three-fourths of the treasure has been discovered. (singular)

Nine-tenths of the eligible workers have registered. (plural)

7. Newspapers, book titles, works of art, or a word spoken of as a word, even when plural in form, are singular.

The Franklin *Times* has a country-wide circulation. (singular)

Trailers is easy to spell. (singular)

8. The nouns *kind, type,* and *sort* are singular.

> The new *type* of frozen foods ordered by our purchasing agent is delicious. (singular)

> The *kind* of skills required to operate heavy construction equipment is often acquired through on-the-job experience (singular)

> This *sort* of grass is recommended by the instructor of our golf-course-management program. (singular)

You may also find some pronouns troublesome when you have to determine their number.

1. Here is a group of pronouns that refer to only one unit (singular): *either, neither, another, each, one, everyone, everybody, no one, anyone, anybody, nobody, someone, nothing, somebody,* and *everything.*

> *Each* of the waitresses has permission to eat her meals in the kitchen. (singular; one waitress)

> *Neither* of the painters enjoys working for a contractor who does not abide by safety regulations. (singular; one painter)

2. The words *none* and *any* may be either singular or plural, depending upon the meaning intended by the speaker.

> None of the employees was hurt. (not one was hurt, singular)

> None of the employees were hurt. (no employees were hurt, plural)

> Any of these boats is safe. (any one is safe, singular)

> Any of these boats are safe. (all are safe, plural)

3. *Some, all,* and *most* may be either singular or plural, depending upon whether they refer to a quantity of something (in which case they would be singular) or to a number of things (plural).

> Some of the money was located by the bank teller. ("Some" is singular.)

> Some of the trees were destroyed. ("Some" is plural.)

> All the pie was purchased. ("All" is singular.)

> All the pies were purchased. ("All" is plural.)

4. *Several, few, both,* and *many* are plural.

> *Both* of the ground-radio operators were informed of the rapidly ap-

proaching weather front.

Many of the air traffic controllers work on weekends.

PRACTICE EXERCISE 11-B

Underline the subject in each sentence. Write *S* beside sentences containing subjects considered as one unit and *P* beside sentences containing subjects considered as more than one unit.

1. Somebody in the laboratory gave the order for the technicians to repeat the blood tests.

2. A truck and a sedan were in the garage.

3. Neither Michele nor Jane wants the position.

4. None of the workers were promoted.

5. No one in our department cares to suggest a solution to the automobile design problem.

6. Most of the lakes were frozen.

7. There are three methods of solving this problem.

8. A number of players have been suspended.

9. Everyone on the police force expects to receive training in first aid and lifesaving techniques.

10. The crowd was unusually quiet.

11. The family have agreed among themselves to vote for the same candidate.

12. Fifty dollars is not enough for six tickets to the game.

13. Mumps is a disease that adult males should avoid.

14. Many a customer has been turned away after closing hours.

15. This type of nails is recommended for roofing jobs.

16. Two-fifths of the voters are planning to oppose the bill.

17. The sum and substance of the President's speech was peace at any price.

18. All of the cars were purchased.

19. *The New York Times* is read by millions.

20. Fifty percent of the park is reserved for wildlife.

21. The number of sightings is increasing.

22. Nine-tenths of the children have been vaccinated.

23. Neither Gary nor his brother services television sets.

24. Macaroni and cheese is the luncheon special.

25. Several of the secretaries were not informed of the new lunch hour regulations.

LEARNING OBJECTIVE

·To use the verb form which agrees in number with the subject of the sentence

You have now reviewed the two major steps necessary for matching verbs to subjects: (1) locate the subject and verb of the sentence, and (2) determine the number (singular or plural) of the subject. However, before you try the exercises on subject-verb agreement, you need to be aware of three general rules for subject-verb agreement.

1. A verb always agrees in number with its subject, not with a predicate noun that follows the verb.

> Our main problem *is* inexperienced technicians. (The subject is *problem*.)

> His senior stenographer and social secretary *are* highly skilled typists. (The subjects are *stenographer* and *secretary*.)

2. When a singular subject is joined to a plural subject by *or* or *nor*, the verb generally agrees with the nearer subject.

> Either the doctor or his two nurses are expected to testify.

3. *Don't* (do not) and *doesn't* (does not) should always agree with their subjects. Use *don't* with the subjects *I* and *you*. With all other subjects, use *doesn't* when the subject is singular and *don't* when the subject is plural.

> You don't appear to be nervous when you are welding steel beams on the top floor.

> He doesn't enjoy flying in rough weather.

> They don't like to work on airplane engines when they are not alert.

You are now ready to test your ability to make the subject and verb agree. To do this you only need to be certain that a singular verb is matched with a singular subject and that a plural verb is matched with a plural subject. These three hints will help you tell whether a verb is singular or plural.

1. Is, was, has, and most verbs ending in a single *s* are singular.

he runs, she thinks, it is

2. Are, were, have, and most verbs not ending in *s* in the present tense are plural.

they run, we think, these are

Exceptions, of course, are verbs used with the singular pronouns *I* and *you*.

I think, you think

3. Always use a plural verb with the pronoun *you*.

you are, you have, you were

If you are uncertain about the plural form of other verbs, consult your dictionary.

PRACTICE EXERCISE 11-C

Underline the correct verb form in the following sentences. Remember three simple steps: (1) locate the subject, (2) determine the number of the subject (singular or plural), and (3) match a singular verb to a singular subject and a plural verb to a plural subject.

1. The construction workers on the other side of the street (was, were) demolishing an old tenement house.

2. The interior designer's responses to our letter (change, changes) everything we decided about the carpeting and drapes.

3. Careers in the building trades and in general construction (appeals, appeal) to people of all ages.

4. The depth of some of these valleys (has, have) not been determined by the surveying party.

5. Each of the key punch operators (has, have) transferred the data correctly.

6. The members of our crew (go, goes) on alert almost every weekend.

7. The new agricultural technician, along with all his soil testing equipment, (was, were) flown to the state capital to receive special training.

8. One of the security guards (was, were) injured during the last prison riot.

9. Somebody (has, have) signaled the aircraft dispatcher to clear the runway for an emergency landing.

10. Both of these safety regulations (have, has) been written by the electronic engineers who are conducting underwater sonar tests.

11. Several of our real estate agents (was, were) involved in the promotion of vacation home property.

12. Some of these samples (are, is) ready to be analyzed by the government meat inspectors to determine whether they comply with moisture and additive requirements.

13. Neither of the positions (requires, require) special skills.

14. Everyone who qualified for the oil production jobs in Alaska (was, were) given a thorough medical examination.

15. A few of the maintenance workers (was, were) left behind to clean up.

16. Either the bank president or your friends in the accounting department (is, are) mistaken about the error in my savings account balance.

17. It (is, are) the insulating workers who will apply fiber glass to the roof.

18. He (doesn't, don't) often obey the directives of his supervisor.

19. There (is, are) two roads leading to the new machine shop.

20. A number of our technicians and machinists (has, have) been summoned to the experimental research facility in Detroit to help improve the fuel injection system.

21. A police officer or an official from the traffic safety committee (are, is) required for the safety talk.

22. Peaches and cream (are, is) my favorite dessert.

23. Where (is, are) the lots you described?

24. Neither John nor Mary (are, is) going to operate the data-processing machine.

25. Here (is, are) the wrenches you ordered for the students in the diesel mechanics course.

26. Our high school class (are, is) going to have a reunion this summer.

27. Four-fifths of his estate (were, was) left to the community college.

28. Statistics 101 (are, is) now being offered to freshmen.

29. Our crew (has, have) agreed to fly the chartered aircraft to the conference on vocational rehabilitation.

30. The number of urban planners at the Chicago conference who advocated rail transportation (is, are) unbelievable.

31. Either Kim or her sister (are, is) going to be offered the new counseling position at the welfare department.

32. The mumps (is, are) a disease that can be prevented.

33. Two-thirds of the security officers working in our city (has, have) been assigned the task of investigating who may be potentially harmful to the President.

34. The tactics employed by the United States Forest Service in fighting major fires (has, have) been compared to military combat operations.

35. Our principal concern (are, is) truck drivers who travel across the United States without sufficient rest.

36. This sort of service (is, are) the result of technical expertise and experienced personnel.

37. Many a boy arrested for petty theft (have, has) been ordered by the juvenile court authorities to pay for the cost of the stolen items.

38. Every man, woman, and child in the central business district (was, were) accounted for by the Census Bureau.

39. The word *diseases* (have, has) always been easy to pronounce.

40. *The New York Times* (have, has) been published continuously for many years.

ANSWERS TO PRACTICE EXERCISES

PRACTICE EXERCISE 11-A

1. candidates   are
2. ranger   was
3. Mr. Berry   has been
4. decision   was
5. nails   are

6. signs   were lighted
7. Everything   was
8. objections   seem
9. ship   was lost
10. faculty   was

PRACTICE EXERCISE 11-B

1. S
2. P
3. S
4. P
5. S
6. P
7. P
8. P
9. S

10. S
11. P
12. S
13. S
14. S
15. S
16. P
17. S

18. P
19. S
20. S
21. S
22. P
23. S
24. S
25. P

ANSWERS TO PRACTICE EXERCISE 11-C

1. were	15. were	28. is
2. change	16. are	29. have or has
3. appeal	17. is	30. is
4. has	18. doesn't	31. is
5. has	19. are	32. is
6. go	20. have	33. have
7. was	21. is	34. have
8. was	22. is	35. is
9. has	23. are	36. is
10. have	24. is	37. has
11. were	25. are	38. was
12. are	26. is	39. has
13. requires	27. was	40. has
14. was		

UNIT 12

Modifiers

This unit explains the different types of words and groups of words used to change—or modify—the meaning of basic sentences. These words, phrases, and clauses are called modifiers because they modify the meaning of sentence parts. Mechanics who add extra power to an automobile engine to make it run faster do something similar, because they change a regular stock car into a *modified* stock car.

When using modifiers, always keep in mind the following basic rule:

Adjectives modify nouns and pronouns.

Adverbs modify verbs, adjectives, and other adverbs.

Here is a brief review of adjectives and adverbs:

Adjectives tell us *what kind* (*red* hair, *small* boy, *large* building), *which one* (*this* coat, *that* notebook), and *how many* (*two* women, *several* students). A proper adjective is derived from a proper noun (*Russian* people, *French* food).

Adverbs are words that tell *how* (carefully, happily), *when* (now, soon, often, then), *where* (here, near, inside), *how much* (very, too, extremely), and *why* (therefore, hence). Remember that adverbs modify verbs, adjectives, or other adverbs.

Adverbs Modifying Verbs

The choir sang *beautifully*. (tells how the choir sang)

He moved *recently*. (tells when he moved)

There is the pencil. (tells where the pencil is)

We need him *greatly*. (tells how much we need him)

Adverbs Modifying Adjectives

An *unusually* large amount of snow has fallen. (tells how large)

He has an *exceptionally* keen mind. (tells how keen)

Adverbs Modifying Other Adverbs

Jim runs *very* fast. (tells how fast)

The boys played *extremely* well. (tells how well)

PRACTICE EXERCISE 12-A

Write *adj.* or *adv.* above adjectives and adverbs in the following sentences. (Do not be concerned about the articles *a, an,* and *the,* which also function as adjectives.)

1. Mary heard an unusually loud noise in the new engine.

2. Jim baked two pies for the Spanish booth.

3. Submit the data sheet to the chief engineer.

4. That drill has a long cord.

5. The solar units are now effective.

6. The car is almost new.

7. We must test the circuits thoroughly and carefully.

8. He talks too much.

9. This candy is especially good.

10. The supervisor made the right decision.

LEARNING OBJECTIVE
•To use the adverb form (-ly)

1. The most common error in using adverbs is failing to use the (*-ly*) form. If you have a problem determining whether to use the (*-ly*) form or not, check to see what the word in question modifies. *If it modifies a verb, an adjective, or an adverb, it will be an adverb and you should use the (-ly) ending.*

The money was divided (equal, equally) between the maintenance personnel. (*Equally* modifies the verb *was divided*, and therefore you should use the -ly form.)

I inherited an (unusual, unusually) large amount of money. (*Unusually* modifies the adjective *large*, and therefore is an adverb using the -ly form.)

I feel (extreme, extremely) well. (*Extremely* modifies the adverb *well*, and therefore uses the -ly form.)

2. Not all adverbs, however, end in -ly. Several adverbs you often use have two forms.

close, closely   fair, fairly   slow, slowly

Often the two forms do not have exactly the same meanings.

He held her close.

Jane listened closely to the instructor.

The day will pass fairly quickly if everyone at the match plays fair.

The driver quickly turned his head when she yelled, "go slow." Slowly he turned and said, "You talk too loud."

Note: **Remember, however, that some adjectives end in -ly.**

scholarly **book**   *daily* **practice**
leisurely **ride**   *kindly* **woman**

Also, remember that a few -ly words may be either adjectives or adverbs.

The *early* **shoppers are offered the best bargains by our sales staff. (adjective)**

We left *early* **in order to check the ducts which had been shaped by the sheet-metal workers. (adverb)**

PRACTICE EXERCISE 12-B

Choose the correct form of modifier.

1. Ron received an (unusual, unusually) small amount of applause.

2. Jackie Gleason looked (odd, oddly) at the other actors.

3. (Heavy, Heavily) made up, she was (unrecognizable, unrecognizably) changed from a (youthful, youthfully) looking woman into an old witch.

4. She read the sign (slow, slowly).

5. The mayor is an (extreme, extremely) tall, skinny man.

LEARNING OBJECTIVE

•To use correctly an adverb or an adjective following the five sense verbs: look, smell, taste, feel, and hear

A second situation which causes difficulty for some students is whether to use an adjective or an adverb following the five verbs relating to our senses: *look, smell, taste, feel,* and *hear.* When these verbs indicate an action of the body, adverbs should be used to describe the action.

> The instructor hears each lesson patiently. (action of the ear)
>
> Mary tastes each recipe carefully. (action of the tongue)
>
> Jim smelled paint distinctly in the workshop. (action of the nose)
>
> They looked at the jewelers' lathe curiously. (action of the eyes)
>
> The shipping clerk felt the cloth cautiously. (action of the hands)

More commonly, however, the five sense verbs *are used as linking verbs which do not express an action of the body.* They link a descriptive predicate adjective to its subject.

> The cookies look delicious.
>
> The water feels hot.
>
> Our barn smells musty.
>
> Your pie tastes good.
>
> His story sounded suspicious.

Note: **If the subject of the sentence is doing the sensing (looking, hearing, etc.), then the word after the verb will take the adverb form. If the subject is *not* actively doing the sensing, use the adjective form.**

> **The horse looked sickly at the mouldy hay. (The horse is doing the looking, and sickly tells how the horse *was looking* at the hay.)**
>
> **The horse looked sick. (Someone else is doing the looking, and sick modifies the noun *horse*.)**

Hint: **If you can add "to me" to the sentence and have it make sense, you use the adjective.**

> **The cookies look delicious (to me). (Adjective)**
>
> **He looked at them suspiciously. (Adverb; the sentence does not make sense if *to me* is added.)**

PRACTICE EXERCISE 12-C

Underline the correct modifier in each sentence.

1. Cecil thought she looked (beautifully, beautiful) in her new nurses' uniform.

2. We can finish this job evaluation (easily, easy) in an hour.

3. The French perfume smelled (sweetly, sweet).

4. Our special order of flowers looked (horribly, horrible).

5. Her description of the well-paid position sounded (suspicious, suspiciously) to those of us who heard the details.

6. In spite of what you may think, I have been driving the bus (careful, carefully).

7. After failing to qualify as a lithographic artist, Jane felt (miserable, miserably).

8. The chief engineer was feeling (angry, angrily) because of our mistakes.

9. The castor oil tasted (bitterly, bitter).

10. If you can think (clear, clearly), you should be able to finish the sales presentation.

LEARNING OBJECTIVE

·To use correctly the six most troublesome modifiers

The use of *bad* and *badly, well* and *good,* and *slow* and *slowly* deserves special attention.

The use of either *bad* or *badly* in the sense of being "ill" or "sorry" is now acceptable in standard English. In formal writing and speaking, however, we should say *Joan feels bad.* (Since *feel* is a linking verb, we use the adjective *bad.*)

Note: Badly **may modify action verbs.**

    The choir sang *badly.*

Well is used as an adverb to describe an action. A person *plays* well, *runs* well, *eats* well, or *drives* well.

Well may also be used as an adjective to mean in good health (she *feels* well), of good appearance (John *looks* well), or satisfactory (all *is* well).

Good is always an adjective. Take special care to use *good* after a linking verb. The coffee smelled *good*. The cake tasted *good*.

Slow is used as an adjective in formal English, but such expressions as "go slow" or "drive slow" are acceptable in informal usage because of their use on highway signs. *Slowly* is always an adverb.

PRACTICE EXERCISE 12-D

Underline the correct modifier in each sentence.

1. The roofers work (well, good) together.

2. Do you think the neighborhood security officers could drive (slow, slowly)?

3. The aircraft dispatcher could not hear (good, well) because of the static.

4. The nuclear reactor operator held up fairly (good, well) during the emergency.

5. Tony said that he feels (bad, badly), but the administrator is requesting him to complete the bank statements.

6. The peaches in the custard went (bad, badly).

7. Ms. Johnson told us that she feels (good, well).

8. After this business trip to Hawaii John looks (well, good).

9. The soloist sang very (bad, badly) last Sunday.

10. Some of the space food tasted (well, good).

LEARNING OBJECTIVE
·To use comparisons correctly

There are three levels, or *degrees*, of comparison: positive, comparative, and superlative.

1. The positive does not actually compare two or more items or persons. (It is "neutral.")

> Mrs. Dees is an intelligent person. (This example does not suggest that Mrs. Dees is more or less intelligent than anyone else.)

2. The comparative degree is used when *two* items or persons are compared.

> Janice is the taller of the two plasterers.

The smaller of those two construction workers is my cousin.

Most adjectives and adverbs of one syllable form the comparative by adding -*er* to the positive.

Our exam was shorter than yours.

Adjectives of more than two syllables, adverbs ending in -*ly*, and some adjectives of two syllables form the comparative by putting *more* or *less* before the positive.

He is less dedicated to excellence than the older diesel mechanics.

She is more talented than I could imagine.

Roger lays carpet more rapidly than his brother does.

3. The superlative is used when three or more items or persons are compared.

Martha is the smartest student in the keypunch operators' class.

Most adjectives and adverbs of one syllable form the superlative by adding -*est*.

Our crew has erected the tallest derrick in the oilfield.

Adjectives of more than two syllables and adverbs form the superlative by putting *most* or *least* before the positive form.

He is the most eager employee we have in the store.

Her design is the most efficient in the mechanical aptitude exhibition.

She is the least excited of the air traffic controllers.

Of the six workers in our section, Mary is advancing most rapidly.

4. Some adjectives and adverbs are said to be irregular because they do not follow the usual methods of forming the comparative and superlative.

	Positive	Comparative	Superlative
Adjectives	bad	worse	worst
	good	better	best
Adverbs	well	better	best
	badly	worse	worst

Note: **Remember to include the word *other* when comparing one thing or person with a group of which it is a part.**

Marvin has a higher shooting percentage than any player on the team. (This example is wrong because Marvin is a member of the team and he cannot have a better shooting percentage than himself.)

Marvin has a higher shooting percentage than any *other* **player on the team. (This example is correct.)**

5. Avoid the double comparison.

>Sherry is more funnier than I am. (incorrect)

>Sherry is funnier than I am. (correct)

>She is the most happiest student in the class. (incorrect)

>She is the happiest student in the class. (correct)

PRACTICE EXERCISE 12-E

Place an X in the blank space beside each sentence that makes an incorrect comparison. Revise each incorrect sentence by writing the correct form above the error.

_____ **1.** Mr. Davidson is the tallest of the two pipefitters.

_____ **2.** My tractor-trailer is longer than yours is.

_____ **3.** Larry is a lot more faster than the other bricklayers.

_____ **4.** Our copier sold better than any other machine in the display.

_____ **5.** His boat is the longest in the show.

_____ **6.** Of the four members of the maintenance crew, Dean has been selected to supervise the more difficult jobs.

_____ **7.** He works more diligently than his business partner.

_____ **8.** Since there were only two applicants, the chief air traffic controller had to decide which one would be the better radar technician.

_____ **9.** I found Mrs. Turner the most cooperative of the two private duty nurses.

_____ **10.** Lake Sagamore has the higher cleanliness rating of any body of water in the entire state.

LEARNING OBJECTIVE
•To recognize prepositional phrases used as modifiers

1. A prepositional phrase is a group of words introduced by a preposition. Common prepositions include:

about	before	by	like	to
above	below	except	of	under
after	beside	for	off	up
against	between	from	on	upon
among	but	in	over	until
at		into		with

Most prepositional phrases are two or three words in length and they end with a noun or a pronoun which is called the object of the preposition.

The cat sits *under the table*.

The car hit the bicycle *with its bumper*.

2. Adjective prepositional phrases modify nouns and pronouns.

A large part *of an electrician's work* is preventive maintenance.

Central is the best community college *for someone like me*.

3. Adverb prepositional phrases modify verbs, adjectives, and occasionally other adverbs.

In the morning my secretary types important business letters before she opens the mail. (modifying the verb *types*)

Jim seems sure *of himself* when he overhauls a transmission. (modifying the predicate adjective *sure*)

Joseph tightened the bolt holding the water pump as far *to the left* as he could. (modifying the adverb *far*)

Note: **Do not be confused by prepositional phrases that function as absolute or independent elements—that is, without any grammatical relationship to the sentence in which they appear.**

Missile assembly mechanics have, *on the whole,* **exhibited a high degree of skill.**

By all means, **send your qualifications to the supervisor for evaluation.**

PRACTICE EXERCISE 12-F

Underline all prepositional phrases.

1. Self-employed paperhangers work directly for property owners on small jobs.

2. The homes on our block were built by a carpentry class from the technical institute.

3. The news about our urban redevelopment project came at noon.

4. Cement masons work principally on large buildings, but many are employed on highway construction projects.

5. Most construction electricians work for electrical contractors.

6. The electrician usually terminates the incoming electrical service into a central fuse box.

7. Tile setters and terrazzo workers are employed mainly in new building construction.

8. Tiles are usually tapped into place with a trowel handle.

9. The demand for terrazzo workers is expected to increase.

10. Growth of the trade will be stimulated by the use of new terrazzo materials.

> *Note:* Participial phrases, adjective clauses, and adverb clauses also function as modifiers. However, these modifying phrases and clauses create little difficulty in writing unless they are nonessential to the basic meaning of a sentence. See Unit 13, page 181 for a discussion of essential and nonessential participial phrases. See Unit 13, pages 179 to 181 for a discussion of essential and nonessential clauses.

ANSWERS TO PRACTICE EXERCISES

PRACTICE EXERCISE 12-A

1. unusually (adv.), loud (adj.), new (adj.)
2. two (adj.), Spanish (adj.)
3. data (adj.), chief (adj.)
4. That (adj.), long (adj.)
5. solar (adj.), now (adv.), effective (adj.)
6. almost (adv.), new (adj.)
7. thoroughly (adv.), carefully (adv.)
8. too (adv.), much (adv.)
9. This (adj.), especially (adv.), good (adj.)
10. right (adj.)

PRACTICE EXERCISE 12-B

1. unusually
2. oddly
3. heavily, unrecognizably, youthful
4. slowly
5. extremely

PRACTICE EXERCISE 12-C

1. beautiful
2. easily
3. sweet
4. horrible

5. suspicious
6. carefully
7. miserable

8. angry
9. bitter
10. clearly

PRACTICE EXERCISE 12-D

1. well
2. slowly
3. well
4. well

5. bad
6. bad
7. well

8. well
9. badly
10. good

PRACTICE EXERCISE 12-E

1. X (*taller* instead of *tallest*)
2. correct
3. X (*faster* instead of *more faster*)
4. correct
5. correct
6. X (*most* instead of *more*)
7. correct
8. correct
9. X (*more* instead of *most*)
10. X (*highest* instead of *higher*)

PRACTICE EXERCISE 12-F

1. *for property owners; on small jobs*
2. *on our block; by a carpentry class; from the technical institute*
3. *about our urban redevelopment project; at noon*
4. *on large buildings; on highway construction projects*
5. *for electrical contractors*
6. *into a central fuse box*
7. *in new building construction*
8. *into place; with a trowel handle*
9. *for terrazzo workers*
10. *of the trade; by the use; of new terrazzo materials*

UNIT 13

How to Use Commas

INTRODUCTION

Inserting commas accurately is of great importance to the career-oriented student. Basic comma errors tend to stand out and give a negative impression of the writer. On the other hand, business letters, memos, or reports with each mark of punctuation properly placed will accurately portray the writer's ideas and will be less likely to be misunderstood.

A special index that includes actual examples of the sentence parts that require commas is provided to help you quickly locate the material you need to solve specific comma problems. For example, many of you may not know what a *statement of contrast* is, but when you see the example of such a statement, you will know what the index is referring to.

      Use scientific data, **not common sense.**

Although the comma is the most troublesome of all punctuation marks, its use may be reduced to four basic rules which are illustrated by the following diagrams:

1. To set off certain introductory elements

    _____, _____.
    To meet the deadline,   we will have to get started next week.

2. To set off nonessential and other parenthetical elements

    _____, _____, _____.
    Our plan of action,   *therefore,*   must follow a firm schedule.

3. To separate items in a series

    _____, _____, _____.
    We should also have goals,   checkpoints,   and a standard of evaluation.

4. To precede conjunctions that join main clauses

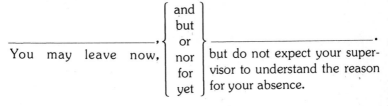

HOW TO USE COMMAS   **171**

SPECIAL INDEX FOR COMMA UNIT

The first diagram, as well as the material in the first part of this unit, is concerned with the various words and groups of words placed at the beginning of a sentence. These introductory elements are in boldface in the examples that follow. Notice how these introductory words and groups of words fit the pattern:

————————————,   ————————————.

    (Introductory element),   (remainder of sentence).

After **servicing intercity buses for five years,** [gerund phrase as the object of the preposition *after*] Ginger decided to apply for the position of assistant service manager.

Your second diagram represents nonessential or parenthetical elements. These are usually placed near the middle of a sentence, although they are sometimes placed at the beginning or at the end of a sentence.

_____,   _____,   _____.

(Basic sentence),   (nonessential element),   (basic sentence).

Drywall plaster, **which was developed after World War II as a substitute for wet plaster,** consists of a thin wall of plaster sandwiched between two pieces of heavy paper.

Mr. Barnes, **cleaning his truck with a special detergent,** was preparing to enter the competition at the State Fair.

The electronic communications center, **a new addition to our campus,** was established in 1977 by Dr. Cecil Norris.

Job openings for ironworkers, **however,** are usually more abundant during the early spring when the weather warms up and the level of construction activity increases.

Use scientific data, **not common sense.**

Ms. Brown, have you seen our new letterhead?

On Monday, January 15th, we went to the stamping plant.

His personality being what it is, [nominative absolute expression] I believe we should compromise.

She arrived early, **didn't she?**

She arrived early, **didn't she!**

Your third diagram represents words or groups of words that appear as a series.

_____, _____, _____, _____.

(Basic sentence),   (series element),   (series element),   (series element).

During the Christmas holidays our yard crew trimmed the trees, painted the front gate, and installed a new roof.

For dinner we had chicken, sweet potatoes, cranberry sauce, peas, and rice and gravy.

It was a warm, sunny afternoon in October.

Your fourth diagram represents main clauses joined by a comma or a semicolon.

_____, _____.

(Main clause),   (and, but, or, for, nor, yet)   (main clause).

_____; _____.

(Main clause);   (main clause).

Either your technical data is not correct, or the computer has made an error.

We asked the supervisor for a raise, but he said that the board of trustees would have to consider a new budget before any salary increases could be approved.

The time trials continued at a hectic pace; all drivers were asked to remain in their cars.

LEARNING OBJECTIVE

•*To punctuate correctly the different types of introductory words, expressions, phrases, and clauses*

This learning objective represents a basic pattern of punctuation which is summarized in the following parts guide:

1. Introductory adverbs
2. Interjections
3. Transitional expressions
4. Adverb clauses
5. Prepositional phrases
6. Phrases containing verbals

main clause

—————————————————, ————————————————————.
↓   ↓

1. The first sentence construction which fits the pattern described above uses the introductory adverb.

> Finally, the rescue party reached the trapped miners after several attempts had failed.

> Fortunately, employment among minority groups has risen during the past six months.

Note: **Decide carefully whether or not to use a comma after an introductory adverb. The comma should *not* be used unless you want to give the introductory adverb special emphasis or unless you want to give the meaning of the introductory adverb more time to "sink in." The following examples are correct without the comma.**

> **Fortunately the paving machine drivers exercised great caution.**

> **Finally the traffic jam of homeward-bound commuters was relieved by a special detachment of highway patrol officers.**

2. You may use a comma after a mild interjection.

> *Oh,* I hadn't heard about his new employment opportunity.

The introductory words *yes* and *no* are usually followed by a comma.

> *Yes,* the urban redevelopment project will be completed by our construction company.

3. When used as introductory elements, transitional expressions are usually followed by commas. Transitional expressions serve as links or "bridges" between sentences and paragraphs.

> *For example,* the working drawings show the exact dimensions of every part of the structure.

> *On the other hand,* I do not believe that your mail delivery truck rides as smoothly as my car does.

> *In fact,* the temperature often goes below zero when we repair the Alaskan pipeline.

4. Introductory adverb clauses are usually followed by commas.

As soon as our assistant completes his training program, he will probably be promoted to sales manager.

While (he was) singing the "Star Spangled Banner," John noticed that a large number of students were talking to their friends. (In this example *he was* may be omitted or understood.)

Exception: When an introductory adverb clause is unusually short or is closely related to the main clause, you may omit the comma.

If we go to the contractor she will be offended.

After John arrived we started sorting out the parts to be used in the carburetor.

If you can, get some strawberries at the corner market. (Here the comma is necessary to prevent misreading.)

You may also omit the comma following introductory adverb clauses when the subject of the introductory clause is repeated in the main clause.

When she comes to the end of Asbury Drive she should turn left and drive two miles past the electronics plant.

Note: When an adverb clause is placed at the end of a sentence, a comma is not usually required.

We waited *until the bus returned from the tour of the industrial park.*

However, such adverb clauses are set off with a comma whenever you want to make a distinct pause, as in the following examples.

The work of plumbers and pipefitters is active and sometimes strenuous, *whether they are working in inaccessible places or standing on a ladder for prolonged periods.*

A large number of plumbers and pipefitters have acquired plumbing and pipefitting skills informally, *although some of them have completed apprenticeship training programs.* **(When such clauses begin with** *although,* **a comma is usually required.)**

5. When several prepositional phrases appear one after another at the beginning of a sentence, use a comma.

In the cupboard on the bottom shelf behind the plates, you can find some spoons.

You may omit the comma, however, if there are only two such phrases and if the sentence reads easily without a pause.

In response to the last statement I can only point to my past record in the railroad industry.

A single prepositional phrase at the beginning of a sentence may also need a comma if the phrase is unusually long, deserves special emphasis, or creates the possibility of a misreading.

> *During those early boyhood years*(,) time seemed to pass very slowly. (This phrase is unusually long, and a comma may be used; however, since the entire sentence is relatively short and can be read easily without pausing, it would also be correct to omit this particular comma.)

> *In desperation,* Congress passed the anti-pollution bill. (special emphasis)

> *To Harry,* James was an exceptionally fine young musician. (possibility of a misreading)

Hint: Remember that single prepositional phrases indicating time or place are not usually followed by a comma.

> *In May* **our electricians from other states will have to pass an examination to qualify for a license.**

> *On Monday* **our instructor will be taking us to observe the bridge construction.**

6. Introductory phrases containing verbals (verb forms that function in some other way), except gerund and infinitive phrases used as subjects, are often followed by commas.

> Because of his tendency *to drive slowly,* Larry won the top-driver award at the trucker's convention. (introductory phrase containing an infinitive phrase)

> To obtain a uniform surface of plaster, the plasterer applies a border of the desired thickness to the top and bottom of the wall section to be covered. (infinitive phrase modifying the verb *applies*)

> *Shrugging his shoulders in an indifferent manner,* the roofer applied another coating of asphalt to the garage. (participial phrase modifying *roofer*)

> After *rigging the heavy construction machinery with the proper cables,* the ironworkers decided to eat lunch and rest for an hour. (gerund phrase as object of a preposition)

> *To become a skilled elevator mechanic* is her ambition. (infinitive phrase as subject—no comma required)

> *Installing and repairing modern elevators* requires a working knowledge of electronics and hydraulics. (gerund phrase as subject—no comma required)

PRACTICE EXERCISE 13-A

Supply the missing commas. Place optional commas inside parentheses. Some of these sentences do not require commas.

1. While she was painting the ceiling she fell from the scaffold.

2. Realizing what he wanted in life Mac went to a technical school on borrowed money and worked as a waiter every weekend.

3. Having covered the entrance to the shopping mall with a special type of outdoor carpet Mr. Daniel discovered that it was not necessary to ask the shoppers to wait until the adhesive was dry.

4. To set up and rig hoisting equipment for erecting and dismantling structural steel frames is the job of riggers and machine movers.

5. Waterproofing existing structures is expected to provide an increasing proportion of roofers' work.

6. In erecting a steel framework structural-iron workers push steel beams into their proper position in the structure.

7. Before the equipment arrived we decided to change the dimensions of the building.

8. To determine the size and type of sheet metal to be used the sheet-metal worker plans the job in advance.

9. During his early childhood years Mr. Smith developed a deep appreciation for working with his hands.

10. Painting and paperhanging are separate skilled building trades although many specialists in these trades do both types of work.

11. If the insulation arrives before lunch you will be able to complete the house this afternoon.

12. Because Jane knew how to install customized kitchen equipment she was selected by the committee to attend the exhibition in St. Louis.

13. To help our committee voted to award William a scholarship.

14. In December the trainees will have completed the courses in drafting and blueprint reading.

15. In response to my last letter Judy said she could not meet the printer's deadline.

16. Modern highway paving equipment results in smoother pavements because electronic grade controls are being used increasingly.

17. In reply to my letter about the prize the awards committee said that I had failed to follow all the rules of the contest.

18. Many highways need repairing after they are used by unusually large vehicles.

19. By the way have you seen the specifications furnished by the architect?

20. Finally Mr. Lanford arrived with the sand and cement.

LEARNING OBJECTIVE
•To punctuate correctly the various types of nonessential interrupting elements in a sentence

The parts guide below represents a summary of the various nonessential interrupting elements:

	1. Nonessential clauses	
	2. Nonessential phrases	
	3. Appositive phrases	
	4. Parenthetical expressions	
	5. Statements of contrast	
	6. Nouns of direct address	
	7. Dates and addresses	
(First part of the *main clause*),	8. Absolute elements	(Remaining part of the *main clause*).
	9. Questioning or exclamatory elements	

As you study each of these constructions or elements, bear in mind several hints that will help identify them.

If you omit any of the constructions or elements listed in the summary above, a complete sentence (or a main clause) will remain.

If you read aloud at medium speed a sentence which contains any of the constructions listed above, you will notice that a slight pause usually occurs both before and after the interrupting elements.

As you study these constructions, notice that they always contribute something extra to a sentence; they provide additional information not needed to complete the basic meaning of the sentence.

1. Nonessential clauses are set off with two commas when they appear in the middle of a sentence and with one comma when they appear at the beginning or at the end of a sentence. A nonessential clause always adds a fact that is not essential to the meaning of the sentence. In the examples below, notice the difference between an essential clause that adds necessary information to the sentence and a nonessential clause that does not.

Mr. Ted Peoples, who played left field for our college baseball team, is employed as a supervisor in a sporting goods store. (Notice that the basic sentence is concerned with stating that Mr. Peoples is a supervisor. That he played left field for a college baseball team is not essential to the meaning of the basic sentence.)

The boy who works as a carpenter's helper is my brother. (In this sentence the clause *who works as a carpenter's helper* is essential to the basic meaning of the sentence because it points out which boy the brother is.)

Modern high-speed elevators, which are usually found in skyscrapers, use electrical and electronic controls. (The fact that high-speed elevators are found in skyscrapers is additional information.)

The ducts you have in your house were installed by a local heating contractor. (In this sentence the dependent clause expresses part of the basic meaning of the sentence.)

Many sheet-metal workers spend considerable time at the construction site, where they may work either indoors or outdoors. (In this example you have a nonessential clause coming last in the sentence.)

Hint 1: Most clauses which modify proper nouns are nonessential and should be set off with commas.

Hint 2: Most clauses beginning with the word *that* are essential and do not require commas. Note, however, the following rare exceptions to this rule:

That Jim Smith was the fastest bricklayer in our crew, no employee could deny.

Tom has given his answer, that his mind is made up.

The committee decided that Mr. Graham would be the speaker, that only employees with tenure could attend, and that the entertainment would be provided by a folk guitarist from Spain.

Some clauses may be either essential or nonessential, depending on the meaning intended by the writer.

The boys took their problem to the mechanic who is an authority on citizen's band radios. (In this sentence the boys could choose to go to more than one mechanic. However, they choose the mechanic who knows about citizen's band radios.)

The boys took their problem to the mechanic, who is an authority on citizen's band radios. (In this sentence the boys could go to only one mechanic, and he happens to be an authority on citizen's band radios.)

2. Nonessential participial phrases are set off with commas. A participle is easy to recognize if you look for words ending in *ing, ed, en, n, t,* or *d,* that function as adjectives (*smiling* face, *drifted* snow). When other words are added to a participle, a participial phrase is formed. The examples below illustrate nonessential participial phrases which add extra information to a sentence and must be set off with a comma or commas.

> *Being the only one to finish the test,* Sam was assigned to the bookkeeping department.

> Mrs. Johnson, *excusing herself quietly,* left the machine shop and went to the shopping center for lunch.

Here is an example of an essential participial phrase.

> The man *fixing my car* is also the service manager.

3. Appositive expressions are set off with a comma or commas. Such expressions usually follow and name or rename another noun. In the examples below, notice that some appositives are essential (no commas are used) and some are nonessential (a comma or commas are required).

> Jim Harris, *a senior at Ferndale,* is planning to go to college.

> His new job, *repairing automobile engines,* required all his spare time. (gerund phrase appositive expression)

> Dick's principal goal, *to qualify for on-the-job training as a radiation monitor,* seems unrealistic at the present time. (infinitive phrase appositive expression)

In the examples that follow, notice that essential (no commas) appositives are usually short and closely related to the word they name or rename.

> My friend Bill is the piano tuner you should call. [*Bill* is a one-word appositive that follows and (re)names the noun *friend.*]

> The novel *Gone with the Wind* was read by millions. (*Gone with the Wind* is an appositive that follows and identifies the noun *novel.*)

> Your cousin Jeanne is a very efficient receptionist. [*Jeanne* is a one-word appositive that (re)names *cousin.*]

4. Parenthetical expressions are often set off with commas, but you should realize that the writer's intention determines the punctuation of a parenthetical expression. If the writer does not desire a pause, omit the commas. Most parenthetical expression occur at the very beginning of a sen-

tence or somewhere in the middle. Any of the nonessential or interrupting elements may be defined as parenthetical expressions, although most instructors commonly think of the following expressions whenever they use the term parenthetical:

I believe (think, know, hope, etc.); on the other hand; on the contrary; also; I am sure; after all; by the way; however; perhaps; moreover; therefore; in my opinion; of course; for instance; to tell the truth; nevertheless; in the first place; that is; etc.

My instructor will, *I am sure,* let me replace the picture tube to gain experience.

To tell the truth, she did not realize that she was accepted for the position with the security force.

We believe, *however,* that he should not be allowed to work in the forge shop without additional training.

Note: **When *however* is used parenthetically, commas are always used to avoid confusion. When *however* means "no matter how," it is not parenthetical and commas are not used.**

However you plead, the judge must still pass sentence.

Now observe a number of examples where parenthetical expressions are used in sentence constructions which do not require commas.

We *therefore* agreed to hire two more operators for the impression-die power hammers.

I am *also* of the opinion that we need another trimmer who is highly skilled in removing excess metal from forged pieces.

Your efforts will *of course* be appreciated by the customers.

He is *perhaps* the best press operator in the forge shop.

5. Use commas to set off statements of contrast.

His father, not his crew chief, is the person to ask.

Our successes, not our failures, should be emphasized.

Use your strength, not a crutch.

6. Set off nouns of direct address (indicating the person or group to whom we are speaking) with commas.

I came, Ken, because you asked me to make a sample cast of the die cavity.

Margaret, are you going to check the furnace temperature?

Are we in agreement, gentlemen?

7. In dates and addresses *every* item following the first is set off with commas.

On Monday, August 10, 1980, we are expected to report to our new duty station.

The Acme Company of 360 Spring Street, Columbus, Ohio, will send you a bill.

Note: **Some authorities allow the comma to be dropped after the year when a complete date is given.**

On Tuesday, November 12, 1980 we shall leave for our vacation.

Note: **When only the month and day or month and year are given, commas are not required.**

It was on June 10 that we began to drill for oil in Louisiana.

In August 1977 we started building.

Note: **When certain items are joined by a preposition, commas are unnecessary.**

He lived at 222 North Main Street in Chicago.

Note: **When only the city and state are given, remember to include a comma before and after the state.**

Atlanta, Georgia, is the transportation hub of the South.

8. Absolute elements (parenthetical expressions that do not have any subordinating conjunctions to link them to the main clause) are usually set off by a comma.

Win or lose, always play by the rules. (absolute phrase)

Her temper being what it is, I feel that we should not tell her the details of the accident. (nominative absolute expression)

9. Use a comma to set off a short clause that changes a statement into a question or an exclamatory sentence.

The vending machine operator arrived this morning, didn't she?

Your secretary is so thoughtful, isn't she!

PRACTICE EXERCISE 13-B

Supply the missing commas. Place optional commas inside parentheses. Some of these sentences do not require commas.

1. The spring quarter begins on March 12.

2. The person who mends tears in worn and damaged clothing is classified as an alteration tailor.

3. Use your brains not your intuition.

4. Their new summer cottage which was built by an independent carpenter is a favorite retreat for their business associates.

5. The students explained their difficulty to the instructor who is an expert at repairing cameras.

6. A truck bearing a Utah license plate was trying to pass us.

7. Our new ranch-style home built by a local contractor is painted green and white.

8. Do you believe that he will arrive on Saturday October 13 1979?

9. My brother Bob checks installed electronic components to ensure compliance with technical specifications.

10. He therefore suggested that we calibrate the aircraft electrical system.

11. Nevertheless our parents have finally decided to buy a small trailer and retire to Florida.

12. Your donation will of course be appreciated by all employees.

13. We sent the package to 123 Maple Avenue in San Francisco.

14. Craig are you driving the radar air controller to the airport?

15. The train dispatcher is coming on December 24.

16. Mary Stevenson a new neighbor has demonstrated her ability to type manuscripts on several occasions.

17. Send your request to 841 Thatcher Avenue River Forest Illinois.

18. They sent the reply to 990 Woodline Drive in Indianapolis.

19. His personality being what it is I do not believe that we should give him our support.

20. Our director is a handsome person isn't he?

21. Pearl Harbor Hawaii was attacked on December 7 1941.

22. The letter was sent to 625 North Street Santa Fe New Mexico.

23. The desk you repaired for us is a genuine antique.

24. On Wednesday January 23 1979 our final exams will begin.

25. Mr. James Moore who spent four years in the Coast Guard is responsible for operating and repairing the radio telephone aboard the new oil tanker.

LEARNING OBJECTIVE
•To use commas to separate items in a series

1. Use commas between the items in a series but not before or after the series (unless a comma is required for some other reason not related to the series).

(Incorrect) During our vacation period the crew installed, a new door, an air conditioning system, and a special greenhouse, in our science building.

(Correct) During our vacation period the crew installed a new door, an air conditioning system, and a special greenhouse in our new science building.

(Correct) After we completed the systems flowchart for the computer, Ms. Tims, Mr. Frazier, and President Robbins waited to see the results of our program. (In this example a comma is used *before* a series to set off the introductory adverb clause, "After . . . computer.")

(Correct) Although the research team found arrowheads, bones, and teeth, there was no conclusive evidence of a settlement. (In this example a comma is used *after* a series to set off an introductory adverb clause.)

(words in a series) Our automobile is clean, quiet, and fast.

(phrases in a series) She ran down the steps, across the porch, and through the yard.

(dependent clauses in a series) Mr. Hoffman explained that we would train personnel in the operation of computers, that we would establish work priorities, and that we would make recommendations for the discontinuance of equipment.

(short, closely-related sentences in a series) We rang the bell, we knocked on the door, and we shouted as loudly as possible. (Such a series is used in imaginative literature to achieve a special effect of style and should be avoided in ordinary writing.)

2. When all the items in a series are joined by *and* or *or,* do not use commas.

We ate beans and rice and corn for supper.

Words thought of as pairs are set off as one item in a series.

For lunch the food service specialist at the rest home served turnip greens, macaroni and cheese, salad, chicken, ice cream and cake, and wine.

3. Do not use a comma between two adjectives when you think of the second adjective as part of the noun it modifies.

> She bought a lovely *gold* watch. (In this example *gold watch* is thought of as a natural pair and no comma is required after *lovely*. See similar examples below.)

> She wore a green *summer dress*.

> We saw a tired *old man*.

> They built a red *brick house*.

> Our son thought he saw a large *wild animal*.

Hint: If two adjectives before a noun do not sound natural when you insert *and* between them, do not use a comma to separate them.

> **a white and frame house (sounds unnatural—no comma)**
>
> **a white frame house**

> **a blue and cotton dress (sounds unnatural—no comma)**
>
> **a blue cotton dress**

> **a handsome and daring young man (sounds natural—use a comma)**
>
> **a handsome, daring young man**

> **a malicious and vindictive old man (sounds natural—use a comma)**
>
> **a malicious, vindictive old man**

4. Newspapers sometimes omit the final comma between the last two items in a series, but do not omit such commas in formal writing, especially if there is the possibility of a misreading.

> They ate bread, beans, rice and honey. (Unless *rice and honey* is a special combination you should use a comma after *rice*.)

> (also correct) They ate bread, beans, and rice and honey.

5. Use a comma before and after *etc.* in a series. (*Note:* The abbreviation *etc.* is not, as a general rule, used in formal writing.)

> All coats, hats, books, etc., should be taken to your locker.

6. Use a comma between two coordinate adjectives that modify the same word or word group. You can ordinarily reverse the order of such adjectives.

> It was a *cold, windy* day. (You could reverse these two italicized adjectives and it would still sound correct to say that "it was a windy, cold day.")

> Kathy wore a long red gown. (A comma is not used in this example because the adjectives are not coordinate. Notice that you cannot reverse the word order and say that Kathy wore a "red long gown.")

PRACTICE EXERCISE 13-C

Supply the missing commas. Some of these sentences do not require commas.

1. After she accepted the job Brenda purchased a planning calendar a special pair of orthopedic shoes and a more economical automobile.
2. Mr. Williams operates the numeric keypunch machine Mrs. Wrenn transcribes data from source material onto punch cards and Ms. Gourley types data on paper tape for input into the data processing system.
3. Melba and Lucy and I were assigned to the shoe department.
4. Your programs texts pencils etc. must be taken to each session.
5. Maxine wore a beautiful fur coat.
6. We hoped for a warm sunny afternoon of golf.
7. Mrs. McDonald served pancakes bacon and eggs coffee orange juice and toast and jelly.
8. The St. Louis Cardinals have an unusually attractive ball park.
9. Your supervisor's happy smiling face was a pleasure to behold.
10. Before attempting to pass all drivers should look to the left to the right and to the rear.

LEARNING OBJECTIVE
•*To use commas and semicolons to join main clauses*

1. Main clauses joined by the conjunctions *and, but, or, nor, for,* and *yet* are separated by a comma. Remember that each main clause can stand alone as a complete sentence.

The campers arrived last night, and the survey party will hike to the top of the mountain tomorrow morning.

Susan is a capable young person, but she has decided to accept a position in a small town.

Some painters may become superintendents on large contract painting jobs, or they may establish their own businesses as painting and decorating contractors.

2. The correlative conjunctions *either . . . or, neither . . . nor, not only . . . but also,* and *both . . . and* are sometimes used to join main clauses.

Either you begin to study every night, *or* your grades will fall below an acceptable standard.

Not only is Mr. Norton a leader in civic affairs, *but* he is *also* president of the board of trustees of our new community college.

Exception: When the main clauses are short or closely related, you may omit the comma, especially if the clauses are joined by *and* or *or.*

The rain must stop soon *or* the graders will not be able to excavate the area according to specifications.

Our crew completed the airstrip *and* we held a special celebration.

We protested *but* the decision was final.

Caution: Before the conjunction *for*, you usually need the comma to prevent a misreading.

We waited several hours, *for* the heavy equipment operators had been delayed by a sudden storm. (Try reading this sentence without the comma and notice how a misreading occurs.)

Caution: Do not mistake a simple sentence with a compound verb for a compound sentence.

The manager was satisfied and gave me a promotion. (simple sentence with compound verb)

The captain received a weather report and changed course. (simple sentence with compound verb)

3. You may also use a semicolon to join two main clauses that are closely related. When we say that clauses are closely related, we mean that both of them make statements about the same subject or about similar subjects.

The weather front was approaching rapidly; all planes were grounded. (Both main clauses have something to say about the adverse weather conditions.)

When you use a semicolon, omit the conjunction.

> The brakes failed to operate; the truck crashed through the fence and turned over three times.

If you have a good ear for the sound of sentences, you will also notice that the rhythm of a sentence with a semicolon is faster than that of a sentence with a comma plus a conjunction. The action described seems exciting and brisk.

> The moment of truth was approaching; we worked furiously to prepare for it.

Caution: **You should not overwork the semicolon. Remember that a semicolon produces a rapid rhythm which can also sound abrupt. If you want your writing to be smooth and free-flowing, the semicolon may be undesirable. In most writing it is preferable to divide your thoughts among separate sentences; use the semicolon only when ideas are so closely related that a period would make too distinct a pause between them.**

PRACTICE EXERCISE 13-D

Supply the necessary commas and semicolons. Some sentences may not require punctuation.

1. Mr. Rowe is going to fly to the textile convention but his wife has decided to take the train that stops in Chicago.

2. The end of the war came swiftly we were not prepared to cope with such a sudden change.

3. Raymond fed the stone into the crushing machine and the driver of the dump truck flashed a caution signal.

4. He wrote the company a second time for the package had been delayed six weeks.

5. Mickey assembled the primer and placed it with the main charge beside the old building.

6. Not only did our section chief direct the pile-driving operation but he also supervised and trained the heavy construction crews.

7. Our feet were nearly frozen the temperature was below zero.

8. The wind blew our roof off and the rain soaked our furniture.

9. The night was dark but we were unafraid.

10. The storm passed quickly we could not believe that our airplane was still flying.

ANSWERS TO PRACTICE EXERCISES

PRACTICE EXERCISE 13-A

1. no comma required
2. life,
3. carpet,
4. no comma required
5. no comma required
6. framework,
7. no comma required
8. used,
9. years(,)
10. trades,
11. lunch(,)
12. equipment,
13. help,
14. no comma required
15. letter(,)
16. no comma required
17. prize,
18. no comma required
19. way,
20. Finally(,)

PRACTICE EXERCISE 13-B

1. no commas required
2. no commas required
3. brains,
4. cottage, carpenter,
5. instructor(,)
6. no commas required
7. home, contractor,
8. Saturday, October 13,
9. no commas required
10. no commas required
11. Nevertheless,
12. will(,) of course(,)
13. no commas required
14. Craig,
15. no commas required
16. Stevenson, neighbor,
17. Avenue, River Forest,
18. no commas required
19. is,
20. person,
21. Pearl Harbor, Hawaii, December 7,
22. 625 North Street, Santa Fe,
23. no commas required
24. Wednesday, January 23, 1979(,)
25. Moore, Guard,

PRACTICE EXERCISE 13-C

1. job, calendar, shoes,
2. machine, cards,
3. no commas required
4. programs, texts, pencils, etc.,
5. no commas required
6. warm,
7. pancakes, eggs, coffee, juice,
8. no commas required
9. happy,
10. pass, left, right,

PRACTICE EXERCISE 13-D

1. convention
2. swiftly;
3. machine(,)
4. time,
5. no punctuation required
6. operation,
7. frozen;
8. no punctuation required
9. no punctuation required
10. quickly;

UNIT 14

Punctuation

Although you may need to work through this entire unit to increase your punctuation skills, you may also find that you need to refer to a specific mark of punctuation only to correct a special problem. The following index is provided for quick reference.

LEARNING OBJECTIVE
•To use the semicolon correctly

1. The semicolon may be used between main clauses that are joined by conjunctive adverbs (adverbs that join or link ideas) such as *accordingly, besides, consequently, furthermore, hence, however, indeed, moreover, nevertheless, thus, therefore, likewise, also, still, then, instead* and by such transitional expressions as *for example, in other words, in fact, on the contrary, on the other hand, for instance,* and *that is.*

   An electronics mechanic in the Marine Corps is trained to diagnose the cause of malfunctions; for example, he uses instruments such as oscilloscopes, ammeters, and voltmeters to locate circuitry defects.

   We were assigned the task of repairing and adjusting orthopedic braces; consequently we were expected to have a knowledge of functional anatomy. (In this example notice that a comma does not follow the word *consequently.* When conjunctive adverbs and transitional expressions follow immediately after a semicolon joining two main clauses, using a comma following such adverbs and expression is frequently optional. Some of these words and expressions create a pause simply because of the way they sound. The expressions *for example, for instance,* and *that is* are almost always followed by a comma.)

Note: Remember that the conjunctive adverbs and transitional expressions listed in this rule often appear at some location other than the beginning of the second clause.

Business pertaining to our lease was discussed; representatives from both parties were therefore required to be present. (In this example the word *therefore* does not create a pause and commas are not required.)

2. Use a semicolon between main clauses that contain several interior commas.

   My brother Burt was handsome, talented, and athletically inclined; and, as a matter of fact, I was somewhat envious of him. (Notice that even though the conjunction *and* is kept in, a semicolon makes the break after *inclined* easy to find. The sentence would be too choppy and too difficult to understand if the reader were confronted with a continuous string of commas.)

3. Use semicolons to separate items in a series that contains interior commas.

   The specialists in our prosthetic laboratory are from Eden, North Carolina; Burlington, Vermont; Milton, Massachusetts; Paradise, California; and Salt Lake City, Utah.

4. Occasionally a semicolon separates one main clause from another main clause in which some words are understood or omitted.

   Concern for the environment is one thing; dedication to free enterprise (is) another. (In this example the verb *is* in the second clause is understood.)

PRACTICE EXERCISE 14-A

Supply the necessary commas and semicolons.

1. It was not possible for us to climb the mountain he pointed out we therefore decided to rest at the base camp for one more day before completing the geodetic survey.

2. The electronic testing equipment from Japan has been reduced however our technical school has decided to purchase it in four separate installments.

3. Your photograph is dirty torn and creased but in spite of these deficiencies our still photographic specialist should be able to reproduce it.

4. The applicants we selected for the management trainee positions were from Minneapolis Minnesota Kansas City Kansas and Cheyenne Wyoming.

5. Belief in a political ideology will not help you get ahead in government service to your country will.

6. Electric sign repairers work in every state however employment is concentrated in large cities and in populous states.

7. All electric sign repairers must be familiar with the National Electric Codes some must also know about the restrictions imposed by local codes.

8. The development of more technically advanced farm equipment which requires greater maintenance will increase the demand for mechanics moreover as the equipment becomes more complex farmers will be less able to make their own repairs and will have to rely more on skilled mechanics.

9. Large numbers of maintenance electricians work in heavily industrialized cities such as Pittsburgh Pennsylvania Chicago Illinois and Akron Ohio.

10. In large shops mechanics may specialize in more than one kind of repair for example some mechanics specialize in major engine repair as well as in automatic transmissions.

LEARNING OBJECTIVE
•*To use the colon correctly*

1. Use a colon before listed items introduced by such words as *the following* or *as follows.*

> We were required to take the following courses: Sociology 201, English 101, Physics 222, and Chemistry 421.

> When you apply for a job at the textile plant, you may need to answer the following questions: Where were you born? When were you married? Who is your employer? Where do you live?

2. Use a colon before a list of appositives:

> The case was large enough for all my hand tools: hammer, square, screwdriver, plane, rasp, drill, and level.

Caution: **The statement that precedes a list of appositives should be grammatically complete.**

(Incorrect) My favorite subjects are: math, spelling, and health.

(Correct) These are my favorite courses: math, spelling, and health.

3. Use a colon before a long and formal statement. The statement may or may not be enclosed in quotation marks.

> President Lincoln's famous speech is known all over the world: "Four score and. . . ."

> Dr. James made the following observation: The time is coming when it will be necessary to use electric cars for short trips.

4. Use a colon to separate main clauses when the second clause explains or restates the idea in the first clause.

> The stock car mechanic from Georgia was exhausted: he had worked for ten hours without a break.

5. Use a colon after the salutation of a business letter, between the chapter number and the verse number of a Biblical passage, between numbers to separate hours and minutes, and between a title and a subtitle.

> Dear Mr. Perry:

> Dear Madam:

> Genesis 3:12

> 9:15 in the morning

> *Economics: An Individualized Course*

PRACTICE EXERCISE 14-B

Add commas and colons to the following sentences.

1. The man from Memphis Tennessee is a superb piano tuner he works on pianos three hours every day and takes special technical courses in New York.

2. In Tommy's desk we found the following items a gold pen two coins some typing paper and a ruler.

3. Dr. Medders suggested a new way of life for his patients It is necessary for you to exercise regularly to eat low calorie foods to cultivate habits of thinking positively and to develop a calm way of living and of working.

4. Have you read *Country Religion The Pure Salvation?*

5. We expect to leave at 730 in the morning.

LEARNING OBJECTIVE

•To use correctly the various end marks of punctuation (period, question mark, exclamation point)

1. Use a period at the end of a statement, an indirect question, or a polite request worded as a question.

> (statement) An audio-video repairer often uses a soldering iron, hand tools, and special testing equipment.

> (indirect question) He asked what the unemployment rate was during the first half of the year.

> (request worded as a question) Will you please pay the bill.

2. Most abbreviations are followed by periods.

> Mr., Ph.D., R.S.V.P., Dr., Ms. or Ms, N.Y.

> **Caution:** The period is often omitted in current usage when the abbreviation refers to a prominent organization or a national agency.

> **IBM, NBC, FBI, UN, VA, CIO, CIA**

3. Use a period after an abbreviated title that follows a name.

> Douglas, Bobbitt, Jr., spoke at our staff meeting on drugs.

4. A period following an abbreviation also serves as the period for the entire sentence.

> I sent the memorandum to Dr. William Daniel, Jr.

5. Use a period after each letter and number in an outline.

> I.
>> A.
>>> 1.
>>>> a.
>>>> b.

6. Three spaced periods (called the mark of ellipsis) are used to indicate an omission of one or more words within a quoted passage. If the omission occurs at the end of the passage, use four spaced periods (three for the omission plus one for the period to end the sentence).

"Surely goodness and mercy shall follow me all the days of my life, and I shall dwell. . . ."

7. A direct question is followed by a question mark.

Who marked the vegetables for our special sale?

Does she plan to hire a secretary? reduce the prices? increase our wages? (Question marks used between the parts of a series give more emphasis to each part.)

8. The exclamation point should be used after strong interjections and after exclamations.

Really! I don't believe we won! What a game!

Caution: **Avoid the overuse of the exclamation point. Mild interjections at the beginning of a sentence are followed by a comma, and mildly exclamatory sentences should end with a period.**

PRACTICE EXERCISE 14-C

Supply the missing commas, periods, question marks, or exclamation points.

1. Well I do not believe he could have finished the valve job on your van

2. Bill Baker Jr asked whether you are going to work for the UN

3. How exciting I just can't believe it

4. What are you going to say when your employer enters the room

5. Will you please change the oil for me

6. Who decides the amount of our annual raise

7. May I borrow your electric drill when you finish the installation

8. The sales meeting was conducted by Henry Smith, Jr

9. Marcia Stevens has completed her PhD

10. Mr. Adams is a serviceperson for ABC

LEARNING OBJECTIVE

·To use quotation marks correctly

1. Quotation marks enclose a person's exact words.

Mr. Anderson said, "You may begin installing the kitchen cabinets next week."

Caution: **Do not use quotation marks to enclose an indirect quotation (not a person's exact words).**

Mr. Anderson said that I could begin working on the kitchen cabinets next week.

A direct quotation begins with a capital letter unless only part of a sentence is quoted.

I heard my music teacher say, "Finish your lesson and practice for two more hours."

Our instructor said the manual was "a ridiculous waste of time." (Only part of a sentence is quoted.)

2. When a quoted sentence is separated into two parts, the second part begins with a small letter.

"Please go," she said, "before I call the police."

Exception: If the second part of a separated quotation is a new sentence, it begins with a capital letter.

"Play quietly," she said. "The miners from the second shift are sleeping."

3. A quoted passage that consists of more than one paragraph requires quotation marks at the beginning of each paragraph and at the end of the entire passage, but not at the end of each paragraph.

Note: **One problem, however, in quoting a passage of several paragraphs is that the quotation tends to merge with the rest of the text and does not stand out clearly as material by another writer. This problem can be eliminated by placing long passages in block form; indent the borrowed material five spaces on both sides and type with single spacing. Omit quotation marks when using block form. The usual rule-of-thumb is to place in block form any quotation that is more than five typed lines or one hundred words long.**

4. Use single quotation marks to enclose a quotation within a quotation.

Abbey recalled her teacher's exact words. "Tomorrow we shall read Sandburg's poem 'Impossible Iambics.'"

5. In dialogue, a new paragraph should begin each time the speaker changes—even if the result is a one-line paragraph.

"Hello, John. How do you like your new job in California?" Terry was trying to be friendly.
"I like it fine," said John.
"Do you have to work on weekends?" asked Terry.

6. Use quotation marks to enclose titles of chapters, essays, articles, short stories, short poems, songs, and other parts of books or magazines. Remember that book titles and names of magazines are indicated by underlining or italics.

7. An excerpt from a poem is enclosed in quotation marks. In informal writing, the quotation marks may be omitted when the author's name is given; in some types of formal writing, however, you must use the quotation marks.

> "To me the meanest flower that blows can give
> Thoughts that do often lie too deep for tears."

> They hand in hand with wandering steps and slow,
> Through Eden took their solitary way.
> Milton

8. Always place periods and commas inside closing quotation marks. Place colons and semicolons outside closing quotation marks.

> I like the poem "Snowbound"; so does Judy.

> "He claims," said Joe, "that you did not deliver the milk on time."

9. Place question marks and exclamation points inside the closing quotation marks when they belong to the quotation. However, when they serve as a mark of punctuation for the entire sentence, place them outside the closing quotation marks.

> "Who was that on the phone?" asked Miss Simpson.

> "Look out!" shouted Tim.

> Did the announcer say, "Jackson scored for California"?

> How I dreaded memorizing "The Highwayman"!

10. Words, letters, or figures spoken of as such are sometimes enclosed in quotation marks in handwritten or typed material. These same items may be italicized in printed material.

> The article "an" is an adjective.

> The letter *b* is not difficult to say.

> The final *o* may be dropped.

11. A quoted question or exclamation may occur in the middle of a sentence.

> The cry of "Help!" could be heard from the second floor.

> The question "Why did I lose?" haunts many of the Olympic participants.

12. Remember to use only one punctuation mark with the closing quotation marks.

> "How long before lunch?", asked Rodney. (In this example the comma should be removed.)

PRACTICE EXERCISE 14-D

Supply the necessary quotation marks.

1. Do you think the word prefabricated is appropriate? asked Mr. Brown.

2. Russell said that we could use the jackhammer to bore holes for charges.

3. Safe! shouted the umpire.

4. Why not, answered the intelligence specialist, we have sufficient information to prepare the situation maps.

5. Did Mrs. Jones say, Patsy can't go to California to look for a job with a movie studio?

6. I shall never learn to appreciate The Hollow Man!

7. What do you think, asked Mark, about the girls in our typing class.

8. Finish your breakfast, said Mrs. Jones. It is time to go to the construction site.

9. I was embarrassed, said Randy, when the teacher told me to sing America.

10. We heard the teacher say, Finish your math exercises and clean up your desk drawer.

LEARNING OBJECTIVE
•To use parentheses and brackets correctly

1. Use parentheses to enclose additional information that is added to a sentence. Notice that a punctuation mark belonging to words coming before parentheses is placed after the closing mark of parenthesis.

> If you decide to visit us (and I hope you do), be sure to bring your set of socket wrenches so that we can finish the tune-up.

2. Complete sentences found inside parentheses need not begin with a capital letter or end with a period, but questions or exclamations inside parentheses should end with a question mark or an exclamation point.

> Carol left yesterday (she had been here for a week) for New York City.

Mr. Baker asked him (what a ridiculous question!) whether he lost his job.

Note: **If a complete sentence beginning with a capital letter is in parentheses, place the period or other end mark inside the closing parenthesis.**

He repeated the order. (The cook did not hear it the first time.)

3. Occasionally, the question mark is inserted into the middle of a sentence to raise doubt in the reader's mind. Similarly, the exclamation point is inserted to suggest shock or surprise. Always enclose such marks inside parentheses.

Soviet Russia is advocating peace (?) on earth.

Note: **Avoid this type of construction whenever the same effect can be achieved without it.**

4. You may use parentheses to mark numbered or lettered divisions within sentences or paragraphs.

Your itinerary will be as follows: (1) Paris, (2) Berlin, (3) Rome, (4) Warsaw, and (5) Moscow.

5. In ordinary compositions you will rarely need to use brackets. However, there are two instances when they may be used: (1) to enclose explanations within parentheses and (2) to enclose an explanation within quoted material when the explanation is not part of the quotation.

"I am proud of it [the new position], but I am aware of the problems that I must face."

"Everyone who knew her [Mrs. Brown] respected her values."

The candidate criticized his own party (we cannot save it [the Freedom party] from destruction) and decided to support the opposition.

Note: **Use a bracketed *sic* to show that an error in quoted material is not an error in quoting, but one that occurs in the original text.**

"After we found the monie [*sic*] the case was solved." (The *sic* after *monie* indicates that the misspelling occurs in the source being quoted.)

PRACTICE EXERCISE 14-E

Place parentheses and brackets wherever necessary.

1. When you complete your training at the technical institute and I hope you will, you will be a qualified draftsperson.

2. Mr. Perry arrived this morning he had been riding the bus for twenty-four hours and went immediately to his hotel room.

3. Martha told us what a speech! about her experience as a Peace Corps volunteer in South America.

4. Your tool case should include the following items: 1 hammer, 2 socket wrench, 3 hack saw, 4 pliers, 5 electrical tape, and 6 screwdriver.

5. "Those of us who remember him Mr. Johnson respected his leadership qualities."

6. "We were aware of it the new community college, but we did not apply until after Christmas."

7. The employee praised his organization (we should be thankful for it the rescue squad) and asked the local newspaper to urge citizens to make a financial contribution.

8. "When you attend the annual company partie *sic* you will meet the assistant manager."

9. After Ms. Brown finishes the technical report preferably before spring vacation, it will be submitted to the board of directors.

10. "Whenever it was received by the pilots the weather report, they made a final decision to depart."

LEARNING OBJECTIVE
·To use the dash correctly

A dash is similar to a comma, but the dash is more forceful and interrupts a sentence more abruptly. Generally, dashes set off parenthetical elements sharply and give them special emphasis.

> That stenographer from Montana—charming and intelligent—has been assigned to the senior engineer in our department. (The adjectives *charming* and *intelligent* are more forceful because of the dashes.)

1. Occasionally you need dashes to set off a series of appositives that might be confused with the noun they explain.

> His three auto mechanics—Kenneth, Bill, and Jimmy—are planning to serve as the pit crew for a famous racing driver. (If the dashes were removed and a comma were placed after *mechanics,* the reader would not know whether three mechanics or six mechanics are planning to serve as the pit crew.

2. Use a dash to set off a series of appositives at the beginning of a sentence or at the end of a sentence.

The house, furniture, automobile—everything must be sold.

The crane operators admired their supervisor's leadership qualities—fearlessness, physical drive, and the ability to make quick decisions.

3. Use a pair of dashes to set off a complete sentence that interrupts the normal order of another sentence.

If you like this article as much as I did—I'm sure you will—you'll want to buy a copy for your assistant lab technician.

4. Use a single dash or a pair of dashes to mark a sudden break or change of thought.

Friend or enemy—speak up, man!

Mr. White told me—but don't quote me on this—that he lost several thousand dollars attempting to establish a successful independent repair service.

5. Sometimes a dash indicates a sudden end to a sentence or hesitation in dialogue.

"But I didn't tell you to—!"

"She—she lost my only toy," cried little Marisa.

6. A dash may take the place of omitted letters.

Have you seen Dr. W— lately?

7. When a sentence that includes a list of items is turned around so that the list comes first, use a dash to separate the listing from the remainder of the sentence.

A slide rule, calipers, a straightedge tool, and a ream of drawing paper—is that all you want?

Caution: **Remember that the dash tends to create an informal style; it should be used carefully and sparingly in formal writing.**

PRACTICE EXERCISE 14-F

Supply the missing dashes.

1. Your sister cultured and talented is the person I want to hire for our travel agent.

2. His three cousins Jim, Bob, and Ben are going to work as carpenter's helpers during the summer months.

3. In judging a riveter we look for certain characteristics quickness, strength, endurance, and dependability.

4. If you believe in vocational education I'm sure you do you will be able to find employment.

5. That worker well, I just can't tell you what he looked like.

6. What do you think of Mr. B?

7. A tire wrench, a flashlight, six quarts of oil, some jump cables, and coveralls does this complete your request?

8. "He he broke my pottery," said the little girl.

9. Bricks, lumber, and nails all these items are costly.

10. Twice and twice was enough I climbed to the top beam to weld the remaining seams.

LEARNING OBJECTIVE

•To use the hyphen correctly

1. A dictionary is helpful in determining whether a word should be hyphenated.

2. Hyphenate compound numbers from twenty-one to ninety-nine. Hyphenate fractions when they are used as adjectives before the words they modify.

> sixty-five dollars   a two-thirds majority

> Two thirds of the union members voted against the regulation. (In this example *two thirds* is a noun and a hyphen is not required.)

3. Use a hyphen to join two or more words that function as a single adjective before a noun, but in general do not use a hyphen to join such combinations following a noun.

> They helped with the door-to-door sales campaign.

> He is a well-known musician.

> Mr. Harris is well known in Oklahoma City.

Exception: If one of the modifying words is an adverb ending in -ly, the hyphen is omitted.

> That is a beautifully made sofa.

4. Do not use a hyphen with most prefixes and suffixes.

unknown   postwar   catlike

5. Use the hyphen with all prefixes before proper nouns and before two-word combinations.

    un-American   anti-Nazi   pro-Canadian
    post-World War II   a non-federally aided program

6. Use a hyphen with the prefixes *ex-*, *self-*, *all-*, and with the suffix *-elect*.

    ex-senator   self-made   all-American   governor-elect

7. Use a hyphen to prevent confusion or awkward spelling.

    re-form prevents confusion with *reform*

    re-collect prevents confusion with *recollect*

    de-emphasize avoids the awkwardness of *deemphasize*

    semi-invalid avoids the awkwardness of *semiinvalid*

    five-dollar bills is different from *five dollar bills*

    ten-year-old boys is different from *ten year old boys*

PRACTICE EXERCISE 14-G

Insert the necessary hyphens.

  1. The ex president of our club insisted on a four fifths majority in order for us to be declared anti American.

  2. He is well known among our membership.

  3. That is a handsomely made blanket.

  4. Send me at least fifty five dollars.

  5. The governor elect decided not to make a speech.

  6. Thirty five students were asked to remain for an after school meeting.

  7. The President elect requested a quietly prepared meal.

  8. Your well planned recruitment program convinced me to reenlist.

  9. Two thirds of the voters rejected the bond issue.

10. Two of our carpenters recovered the leaky roof.

LEARNING OBJECTIVE

·To use correctly the apostrophe in forming possessives

1. Add an apostrophe and an *s* to form the possessive of a singular noun, a plural noun not ending in *s*, and an indefinite pronoun.

the man's hat   the witness's comments

the boss's car   Rebecca's dress   (singular nouns)

Mr. Harris's boat

2. Form the possessive of plural nouns ending in *s* by adding the apostrophe alone. Also add the apostrophe alone to form the possessive of singular nouns that end in *s* if the addition of an extra syllable would make the word hard to pronounce.

ladies' hats
attorneys' offices   (plural nouns ending in *s*)

They saw Jesus' robe.   (*Jesus's* and *Phillips's*

Miss Phillips' election   would be hard to pronounce)

3. *My, his, hers, its, ours, yours,* and *theirs* never require an apostrophe to show possession.

The victory is yours. (not your's)

The dog wants its dinner. (not it's)

4. Only the last word shows the possessive form in compound nouns, names of business firms, and two nouns showing joint ownership.

father-in-law's house

mother-in-law's hats   (compound nouns)

secretary-treasurer's report

Sears Roebuck's insurance plan
Roy Searcy and Company's products   (business firms)

Tommy and Pete's dog   (joint ownership)

5. Whenever two or more persons possess something individually, each of their names takes the possessive form.

   Betty's and Elizabeth's slacks were the same color. (individual ownership)

LEARNING OBJECTIVE

•To use correctly the apostrophe in forming possessive adjectives, in indicating omissions, and in forming certain plurals

1. When the words *minute, hour, day, week, month,* and *year* are used as possessive adjectives, an apostrophe is required.

   a minute's rest, five minutes' rest

   a week's work, two weeks' work

2. Words indicating amount in cents or dollars, when used as possessive adjectives, also require apostrophes.

   one cent's worth of candy, three cents' worth

   one dollar's worth, two dollars' worth.

3. Use an apostrophe to indicate where letters have been omitted in a contraction or where numbers have been omitted a date.

   Don't may be used in place of *do not.*

   Class of '42 may be used in place of *class of 1942.*

   It's may be used in place of *it is.*

   Note: Students often confuse the contraction *it's* with the possessive form *its* (its place) and the contraction *there's* with the possessive form *theirs.* Remember that *it's* always means *it is* and *there's* always means *there is*.

4. Use the apostrophe plus an *s* to form the plural of letters, numbers, and words referred to as words.

   Tennessee is spelled with four *e's,* two *s's,* two *n's,* and one *t.*

   We counted fourteen *and's* in that paragraph.

   He wrote two *8's* on the board.

PRACTICE EXERCISE 14-H

Supply the missing apostrophes.

1. Marthas dress is red, white, and blue.

2. Womens clothing is unusually expensive this spring.

3. Everybodys hat is the same color.

4. We have earned three weeks vacation.

5. He bought five cents worth of candy.

6. Its not necessary to insert those ss in the next example.

7. The girls coats are in my mother-in-laws car.

8. The cat wants its ball of yarn to play with.

9. Jesus father was a carpenter.

10. John Jones and Companys products are nationally advertised.

ANSWERS TO PRACTICE EXERCISES

PRACTICE EXERCISE 14-A

1. out;
2. reduced: however(,)
3. dirty, torn, and creased,
4. Minneapolis, Minnesota; Kansas City, Kansas; and Cheyenne,
5. government;
6. state; however,
7. Codes;
8. equipment(,) maintenance(,) mechanics; moreover, complex,
9. Pittsburgh, Pennsylvania; Chicago, Illinois; Akron,
10. repair; for example,

PRACTICE EXERCISE 14-B

1. Memphis, Tennessee, tuner:
2. items: pen, coins, paper,
3. patients: regularly, foods, positively,
4. *Religion:*
5. 7:30

PRACTICE EXERCISE 14-C

1. Well, van.
2. Baker, Jr., UN.
3. exciting! it!
4. room?
5. me.
6. raise?
7. installation.
8. Jr.
9. Ph.D.
10. ABC.

PRACTICE EXERCISE 14-D

·1. "Do . . . 'prefabricated' . . . appropriate?"
2. no quotation marks required
3. "Safe!"
4. "Why not," "we . . . maps."
5. "Patsy . . . studio"?
6. "The Hollow Man"!
7. "What . . . think," "about . . . class?"
8. "Finish . . . breakfast," "It . . . site."
9. "I . . . embarrassed," "when . . . 'America.' "
10. "Finish . . . drawer."

PRACTICE EXERCISE 14-E

1. (and I hope you will)
2. (he had been riding the bus for twenty-four hours)
3. (what a speech!)
4. (1) (2) (3) (4) (5) (6)
5. [Mr. Johnson]
6. [the new community college]
7. [the rescue squad]
8. [*sic*]
9. (preferably before spring vacation)
10. [the weather report]

PRACTICE EXERCISE 14-F

1. sister—cultured and talented—
2. cousins—Jim, Bob, and Ben—
3. characteristics—
4. education—I'm sure you do—
5. worker—
6. B—
7. coveralls—
8. "He—
9. nails—
10. Twice—and twice was enough—

PRACTICE EXERCISE 14-G

1. ex-president, four-fifths, anti-American
2. no punctuation required
3. no punctuation required
4. fifty-five
5. governor-elect
6. Thirty-five, after-school
7. President-elect
8. well-planned, re-enlist
9. no punctuation required
10. re-covered

PRACTICE EXERCISE 14-H

1. Martha's
2. Women's
3. Everybody's
4. weeks'
5. cents'
6. It's, s's
7. girls'; mother-in-law's
8. correct
9. Jesus'
10. Company's

UNIT 15

Mechanics

This unit may serve either as a reference unit in solving individual problems or as a complete unit of instruction on the skills and form of mechanics. Refer to the index below to find what you need to help you use the appropriate forms.

LEARNING OBJECTIVE
·To abbreviate correctly

1. The following personal titles are abbreviated before a personal name.

    Mr.   Mrs.   Ms. or Ms   Dr.   St. (saint)

Words such as doctor or saint should be spelled out when they are not followed by a proper name.

The doctor has been called.

She is a saint.

Abbreviations such as Rev., Hon., Sen., Rep., Gen., Prof., Capt., and Col. may be used before full names or before initials and last names, but not before last names only.

Sen. Jane Lee Black *not* Sen. Black

Prof. R. B. Jones *not* Prof. Jones

Hon. James Edwards *or* the Honorable James J. Edwards *not* Hon. Edwards

Rev. J. R. Jackson *or* the Reverend John Rucker Jackson *not* Rev. Jackson

2. In formal writing spell out names of states, countries, days of the week, months, and units of measure. (*Note:* Units of measure are generally abbreviated in technical writing.)

feet *not* ft.   Sunday *not* Sun.   Alabama *not* Ala.

ninety-two pounds *not* 92 lbs.   United States *not* U.S.

twenty-four millimeters *not* 24 mm

3. In formal writing spell out Street, Road, Avenue, Park, Mount, River, Company, and similar words used as part of proper names.

Beech Street *not* Beech St.

Park Avenue *not* Park Ave.

Mount Mitchell *not* Mt. Mitchell

Ford Motor Company *not* Ford Motor Co.

4. Spell out first names.

George Johnson *not* Geo. Johnson

James Preston *not* Jas. Preston

5. Spell out the words *volume, chapter,* and *page.*

chapter 10 *not* chapt. 10

page 3 *not* p. 3

6. The following abbreviations for certain Latin expressions may be used to indicate common English terms:

i.e. (that is), e.g. (for example), viz. (namely), cf. (compare)

vs. (versus), etc. (and so forth)

Caution: Use *etc.* sparingly in normal writing.

7. After proper names the following abbreviations are acceptable: Jr., Sr., Esq., and degrees such as M.D., Ph.D., Th.D., M.A., and D.D.

8. For dates, or with numbers indicating time, use the following:

A.D., B.C., A.M. (or a.m.), P.M. (or p.m.)

9. Certain organizations and government agencies which are usually referred to by their initials may be abbreviated.

CIO, CIA, DAR, GOP, FBI, AMA, NASA, FHA, TVA

Exceptions: Many abbreviations are acceptable in footnotes and special types of technical writing. In such instances you should follow the directions of your instructor.

LEARNING OBJECTIVE

·To use numbers correctly

1. A sentence should not begin with a numeral.

> (incorrect) 10 boys volunteered for the project.

> (correct) Ten boys volunteered for the project.

2. Spell out numbers that require only one or two words and use figures for numbers requiring three or more words.

> twenty dollars, forty years, ten million, two billion

> 126   1021   2,400,000

Exception: In technical, scientific, mathematical, or statistical writing, most numbers are written as figures.

3. Be consistent in spelling out numbers or in using figures.

> (incorrect) My sister earns forty-two dollars a week and I earn only $36.00.

> (correct) My sister earns forty-two dollars a week and I earn only thirty-six.

4. Endings such as *-st, -nd* or *-d, -rd* or *-d,* and *-th* should not be added to the day of the month when the year follows.

> (incorrect) July 1st, 1934.

> (correct) July 1, 1934.

Also correct:

> On July 1 he began his duties as a dispatcher for the delivery company.

> The first of July we are leaving for Canada to work on the pipeline.

> On July first she shall begin summer school.

5. In ordinary writing, numbers such as 1st, 24th, or 33rd should be written out.

> She was the first in her class.

> He was the thirty-third President of the United States.

However, it is correct to use 24th, 86th, 92nd, etc., when writing the name of a street.

> She lives in the apartment on 87th Street.

6. Figures should be used for street numbers, for divisions and pag book, for percentages and decimals, and for the hour of the day whe with A.M. or P.M.

>She lives at 113 North Main Street.

>That plywood is exactly 0.72 inch thick.

>We are paying 5 percent interest.

>Read from page 40.

>They left at 4:30 A.M.

PRACTICE EXERCISE 15-A

Correct all errors in the use of abbreviations and numbers.

1. My bro. moved to Ga. and now resides at twenty-three James St. Atlanta.

2. Since he was born on Nov. 2nd, 1969, Henry was 3rd in line.

3. Mr. Melvin Barnes is scheduled to read the 5th chap. of the safety manua before the employees in our division at 5:00 P.M.

4. 15 of my friends earn more than seventy-five dollars a week, but I do not earn more than $50.00 a week.

5. Mr. Jackson explained that four-thousand and six new automobile assembly line workers were hired during the past decade.

LEARNING OBJECTIVE
•To capitalize words according to standard usage

No simple set of rules determines whether or not a word or phrase should be capitalized. Instead, there are only guidelines which change according to the times. Regularly capitalized words, however, will be indicated in your dictionary. Therefore, to determine if a particular word should be capitalized, check your dictionary first. Then, review these general rules.

1. The first letter of a sentence should be capitalized.

>Once upon a time. . . .

2. The first word of a direct quotation should be capitalized.

>Her answer was, "We are not going."

>Mary said, "This pie is delicious," and held out her hand for more.

"Do you see that jet?" asked Alan. "Sometimes my father goes to New York on that same plane."

Note: Do not capitalize the first word of a sentence fragment used in a direct quotation. Also, the second part of a broken or split quotation does not begin with a capital letter unless some other rule causes it to be capitalized.

The Fifth Amendment says that no one can be forced "to be a witness against himself."

"Have you," she asked, "really been waiting for me all this time?"

"Mary," he said, "John is coming tonight."

3. The first word of a complete sentence following a colon should be capitalized. Informal writing does not require the first word following a colon to be capitalized.

The following statement was released by the President's secretary: For reasons disclosed by the CIA. . . .

4. Capitalize nouns that name specific geographical locations, but do not capitalize these same nouns when they do not name a specific location.

Upson County	a county in Georgia
Wake Island	an island in the Pacific
Arctic Ocean	an ocean in the North
Glacier National Park	a park in the West
Great Smoky Mountains	a mountain in Tennessee
New York City	a city in New York

Note: Capitalize *city* only when it is part of the official name of the city or a fanciful title.

the Windy City   Salt Lake City   the city of Los Angeles

5. Compass directions that name a definite section of the country or the world should be capitalized. These same words should not be capitalized when they indicate direction.

the South	He lives on the south side of Chicago.
the Middle West	Jim is traveling west.
the Near East	They live east of the mountains.
the Northwest	She is facing northwest.

Note: **The modern trend is to write nouns and adjectives derived from** *East, West, North,* **and** *South* **with small letters; however, it is not incorrect to capitalize them.**

a northerner   southern hospitality   middle-western speech

Adjectives which indicate direction are not capitalized unless they are part of the name of a country.

> southern Virginia   eastern China
>
> West Germany   North Vietnam

Exception: These adjectives are generally capitalized when they refer to a political region.

> Eastern Europe   Southeast Asia

6. Mother, father, sister, brother, cousin, aunt, and uncle are capitalized when they are used with a person's name unless they are preceded by a possessive noun or pronoun.

> Uncle Bill   Cousin David   Brother Harold
>
> his father   Jim's sister   my cousin Bert

7. Capitalize the names of specific streets, highways, buildings, and organizations; significant events; important laws and documents; holidays; special vehicles of transportation; exact names of government bodies; and legally registered corporate names.

> Forty-sixth Street (the second half of a hyphenated street is not capitalized)
>
> Ohio Turnpike, First Avenue, Oak Street, New York Parkway
>
> Astrodome, Grand Central Station, Wrigley Field (buildings)
>
> the Russian Revolution, the War between the States, World Series, Senior Prom (significant events)
>
> Republican party, Sophomore Class, Young Women's Christian Association (organizations)
>
> First Amendment, Taft-Hartley Act, Declaration of Independence, Apostles' Creed (laws and documents)
>
> Fourth of July, Memorial Day, New Year's Day (holidays)
>
> *Peanut I, Queen Mary, Southern Express, Air Force I* (special vehicles of transportation)
>
> Department of Transportation, Indiana State Legislature (exact names of government bodies)

Kent and Sons, General Motors, Coca-Cola, Crest toothpaste (legally registered corporate names)

8. Capitalize a person's name; governmental, military, religious, and academic titles preceding a person's name; and some important official titles when they take the place of a person's name. Do not capitalize occupational titles, even when they precede the name. State or local titles, most military titles, and civilian titles are lower-cased when they take the place of the name.

Robyn Stoner

Robert Smith, Jr. (an abbreviation following a name is also capitalized)

historian Susan Doe

President Millard Fillmore, the President

Senator Edward Kennedy, the Senator, *but* a senator

Governor Hugh Carey, the Governor, *but* a governor

Pope Paul, the Pope, *but* a pope

Ambassador Young, the Ambassador, *but* an ambassador

General MacArthur, the general

Mayor Robertson, the mayor

Note: **Titles that follow a name should begin with small letters unless the person is extremely important.**

Charles Jackson, superintendent of schools

Robert Benton, professor of geography

Henry VIII, King of England

Jimmy Carter, President of the United States (*President* **is usually capitalized when it refers to the head of a nation.** *Vice President* **requires two capital letters when it refers to the Vice President of a nation.**)

9. Do not capitalize *ex, elect, former,* and *late* when the words are used with a title.

ex-Senator, the Governor-elect, the late President Kennedy

10. The first word and all other words except *a, an, the,* and prepositions and conjunctions are capitalized in the titles of books, magazines, articles, long and short plays, songs and long musical compositions, motion pictures, famous paintings, long and short poems, and radio and television pro-

grams. Observe that it is generally true that the longer items appear in italics (underlined when typing) and that shorter items are enclosed in quotation marks.

The Total Woman, Gone with the Wind, Roots (books)

Better Homes and Gardens (magazine)

"A New Reading Program" (article)

Macbeth (play)

"Yankee Doodle" (song)

The Sound of Music (long musical composition)

Patton (movie)

Guernica (famous painting)

The Prelude (long poem)

"Never Seek to Tell Thy Love" (short poem)

"Morning Devotions" (radio program)

"All in the Family" (television program)

11. Religious words referring to a single Deity are capitalized.

God, Heavenly Father, Jesus Christ, Messiah, Almighty, Jahveh, Yahweh, Jehovah, Lord, Master, Saviour

Specific names of other gods are capitalized, but general reference to them are not.

Astarte, Zeus, *but* gods of ancient Greece

Pronouns referring to the Deity are generally not capitalized if the reference is clear.

God in his infinite majesty

but Blessed is the man who trusts in Him

Capitalize books and divisions of the Bible (Old Testament, Psalms), words that take the place of the Bible (Scriptures), and names of churches (First Methodist Church *but* a Methodist church).

12. Words derived from proper names are usually capitalized.

Georgian, American, African

13. Both parts of a hyphenated word are capitalized if each part would be capitalized separately.

Spanish-American, Anglo-Saxon, *but* un-American, God-given

14. The interjection *O* is always capitalized and is never followed by a mark of punctuation, while the interjection *oh* is capitalized only at the beginning of a sentence and is always followed by a mark of punctuation.

Thou wert with me, O Lord.

Oh! I forgot my jack.

15. In the names of newspapers and magazines, *the* is not capitalized unless it is part of the title.

the *Ladies Home Journal*

The News and Observer (*The* is part of the title)

16. Do not capitalize school or college courses unless they are followed by a number or unless a language is named.

mathematics, typing, physical education

college preparatory English

Electronics 210, Economics 52, Sociology 285

PRACTICE EXERCISE 15-B

Circle each small letter that should be capitalized.

1. "praise the lord!" shouted the minister.

2. The apostles' creed is not part of the scriptures.

3. *A farewell to arms* was written by hemingway.

4. Have you read *paradise lost,* a long poem by John Milton?

5. "Never seek to tell thy love" was a short poem studied by girls in the junior class.

6. Did you watch *macbeth* on television last saturday?

7. June said, "this university is charming," and continued her speech to the student group.

8. "John," she said, "are you going to the city?"

9. My daddy is a great man.

10. She is responsible for organizing un-American activities in the north.

11. "Morning devotions" is a special program sponsored by the first baptist church on sixty-eighth street.

12. The michigan state legislature decided not to meet during the winter.

13. Mr. George Smith, president of hamilton motor company, decided to run for president of the united states.

14. Jack Wilson, superintendent of schools, attended stanford university and became president of the senior class on january 16, 1923.

15. The great smoky mountains are located in the south.

16. Ask professor Jones if he would speak to us about the litter problem in upson county.

17. The 1980 world series may be sponsored by coca-cola.

18. My schedule includes, typing, physical education 300, spanish, journalism, european history, and college preparatory english.

19. Jerry jones lives in an apartment building on maple avenue.

20. Our class hopes to read act II of Shakespeare's *hamlet* before the easter holidays.

21. The wrigley building is located on the east side of the city of chicago near eighty-seventh street.

22. john kennedy, our late president, was in favor of the thirteenth amendment and opposed to the taft-hartley act.

23. I think a trip to europe on the *queen elizabeth 2* would be exciting if we could arrive in northern england.

24. Former president Truman enjoyed reading war stories and writing articles on American history.

25. Ask the doctor if he is a member of the republican party.

26. The red cross drive was important to the soldiers of the Korean war.

27. Henry ford, former president of ford motor company, was a personal friend of george Vi, king of England.

28. Next summer we shall visit the birthplace of William Wordsworth, former poet laureate of England.

29. We visited a park in the western part of the state of South Dakota.

30. The carpentry course was developed by James Jones, president of western technical institute.

LEARNING OBJECTIVE

·To underline correctly

1. All words that are underlined when writing in longhand or when typing are set in italic type by a printer.

> (typewritten) <u>Martin Eden</u> was written by Jack London.

> (italics) *Martin Eden* was written by Jack London.

2. Titles of books, magazines, brochures, bulletins, newspapers, musical works, motion pictures, famous works of art, and long poems and plays are underlined (italicized).

> Have you read *Future Shock?*

> Do you subscribe to *The News and Observer?*

> Have you seen *Gone with the Wind?*

> The *Mona Lisa* is in Paris.

> I enjoyed reading *Today's Education.*

Exception: Neither italics, underlining, nor quotation marks are used in referring to the Bible and its parts.

> The second part of the Bible, the New Testament, begins with Matthew.

Note: When the words *a, an,* and *the* appear immediately before a title, they are not underlined (italicized) unless they are part of the title. Underlining (italics) is not used for the name of the city in the title of a newspaper unless the city name is part of the official title.

> **We read** *The History of the World.*

> **Have you seen the** *TV Guide?*

> **Do you read the Greensboro** *News?*

> **I enjoy reading** *The New York Times.* **(exception;** *The New York* **is part of the official title)**

3. Underline (italicize) words referred to as words, letters referred to as letters, and numbers referred to as numbers.

> The final *e* in the word *guide* is silent.

> The first *5* in my serial number is easy to remember.

Note: In typed or handwritten material these items are sometimes enclosed in quotation marks.

4. Foreign words and phrases are usually underlined (italicized) unless they have become part of the English language.

> We wished them *bon voyage*.

> The building has an interesting facade. (no italics for facade)

5. The names of ships, trains, and aircraft are underlined (italicized).

> The original *Queen Mary* is no longer in service.

> Lindbergh's *Spirit of St. Louis* is now hanging in a museum.

PRACTICE EXERCISE 15-C

Underline wherever necessary.

1. I read the Chicago Tribune while I waited for the Denver Express.

2. Mary Ann's remark was a faux pas.

3. The word rhythm is difficult to spell.

4. Interesting articles may be found in the Reader's Digest.

5. Did you enjoy The Sound of Music?

6. Jimmy Carter's campaign airplane was called Peanut I.

7. The Northern Star, an oil tanker operating out of Alaska, was often used to slash through the ice in the harbor.

8. Newsweek often contains articles about the energy crisis.

9. The Spanish word for store is tienda.

10. The letters D.C. are always capitalized when they stand for the District of Columbia.

ANSWERS TO PRACTICE EXERCISES

PRACTICE EXERCISE 15-A

1. brother, Georgia, 23 James Street
2. November 2, third
3. fifth chapter
4. Fifteen, fifty dollars
5. 4006

PRACTICE EXERCISE 15-B

1. Praise, Lord
2. Apostles' Creed, Scriptures

3. *Farewell, Arms,* Hemingway
4. *Paradise Lost*
5. Seek, Tell, Thy, Love, Junior Class
6. *Macbeth,* Saturday
7. This
8. correct
9. correct
10. North
11. Devotions, First Baptist Church, Sixty, Street
12. Michigan State Legislature
13. Hamilton Motor Company, President, United States
14. Stanford University, Senior Class, January
15. Great Smoky Mountains, South
16. Professor, Upson County
17. World Series, Coca-Cola
18. Physical Education, Spanish, European, English
19. Jones, Maple Avenue
20. Act, *Hamlet,* Easter
21. Wrigley Building, Chicago, Eighty, Street
22. John Kennedy, President, Thirteenth Amendment, Taft-Hartley Act
23. Europe, *Queen Elizabeth 2,* England
24. President
25. Republican
26. Red Cross Drive, War
27. Ford, Ford Motor Company, George VI, King
28. correct
29. correct
30. Western Technical Institute

PRACTICE EXERCISE 15-C

1. *Tribune, Denver Express*
2. *faux pas*
3. *rhythm*
4. *Reader's Digest*
5. *The Sound of Music*
6. *Peanut I*
7. *Northern Star*
8. *Newsweek*
9. *tienda*
10. *D.C.*

Glossary

Absolute expression, phrase. An absolute expression has a thought relationship, but no grammatical relationship, with the remainder of the sentence in which it appears. An absolute phrase usually consists of a noun or pronoun and a participle: *Breakfast being finished,* we cleaned the table and washed the dishes.

Adjective. An adjective modifies a noun or pronoun by telling what kind (*Chinese* dish), which one (*fourth* floor), how many (*ten* acres), or what color (*black* hair). An adjective may be a single word (*beautiful* woman), a phrase (man *of great strength*), or a clause (tool *that I borrowed from the supervisor*).

Adverb. An adverb modifies a verb, an adjective, or another adverb by telling when (come *now*), how (walk *quietly*), where (*here* is the mail), or how much (*very* cold). An adverb may be a single word (ran *fast*), a phrase (rain fell *on the parched fields*), or a clause (he will pay the bill *when you send it*).

Antecedent. An antecedent is the noun or noun phrase that a pronoun refers to or "stands for."

The *carpenter* who built our home is in partnership with his father. (*Carpenter* is the antecedent of *his*.)

Owning a vacation home has its advantages. (*Owning a vacation home* is the antecedent of *its*.)

Appositive. An appositive is a noun or a noun phrase that identifies another noun or pronoun immediately preceding it.

We *plumbers* ought to receive a raise. (appositive)

Ms. Jones, *our purchasing agent,* would like to explain your duties. (appositive phrase)

Articles. The articles (*a, an, the*) may be classed as adjectives because they have limiting or specifying functions. *A* and *an* are indefinite articles; *the* is the definite article; *a* hammer, *an* error, *the* physician.

Auxiliary verbs. Auxiliary verbs are "helping" words that accompany other verb forms to indicate tense or mood or voice. The italicized words are auxiliary verbs:

She *will* walk to work. He *is* walking to town. He *has* worked here before.

He *has been* walking to work. He *could have been* promoted.

Case. A case is one of the forms that a noun or pronoun takes to indicate its relation to other words in the sentence. There are only three cases in English: nominative, possessive, and objective. A noun or pronoun is in the nominative case when it indicates the person or thing acting, in the possessive case when it denotes the person or thing owning or possessing, and in the objective case when it indicates the person or thing acted upon.

Clause. A clause is a group of related words which has a subject and a predicate. An independent (or main) clause may stand alone as a simple sentence. A dependent (or subordinate) clause also contains a subject and a predicate but cannot stand alone because it does not express a complete thought.

Clarity. Clarity means orderliness (directness) of thought and of written expression.

Coherence. In a paragraph, coherence means that all the sentences express ideas which are clearly and logically related to one another. In a sentence, coherence means that all the words are placed to achieve clear communications or a desired emphasis.

Comma splice.   A comma splice is the use of a comma instead of a coordinating conjunction or a semicolon between the two main clauses of a compound sentence.

Comparison.   Comparison refers to the forms of an adjective or adverb that indicate degrees in quality, quantity, or manner.

Complement.   A complement is the word or phrase, following a verb, that "completes" the predicate of a clause. A complement may be (1) the direct object of a verb, (2) a noun or noun phrase following the verb *to be*, or (3) an adjective following the verb *to be* or a linking verb.

He hit the *ball*. (direct object)   He is an excellent *student*. (predicate noun)

She is *happy*. (predicate adjective)   The candy tastes *sweet*. (predicate adjective)

Complex sentence.   A complex sentence consists of one main clause and one or more dependent clauses.

Compound sentence.   A compound sentence consists of two or more main clauses.

Compound-complex sentence.   A compound-complex sentence contains two or more main clauses and one or more dependent clauses.

The game is postponed when it rains, but the players are asked to wait in the dugout.

Conjunction.   A conjunction is a linking word used to connect words or groups of words in a sentence. Conjunctions are of two main kinds: coordinating conjunctions, such as *and, but, for, or, nor,* which join words or groups of words of equal rank; and subordinating conjunctions, such as *if, since, because, as, while, so that, although,* or *unless,* which join dependent clauses to main clauses.

Certain conjunctions used in pairs are called correlative conjunctions. The most frequently used of these are *both . . . and, either . . . or, neither . . . nor, so . . . as, whether . . . or, not only . . . but also.*

Contraction.   A contraction is a shortened form of a word in which an apostrophe indicates the omitted letters, such as *don't* for *do not, can't* for *cannot,* and *I'll* for *I will* or *I shall.*

Dangling modifier.   A dangling modifier is a group of words that is not attached to a word in a sentence or that is attached to the wrong word.

By leaving now, the heavy traffic can be avoided. (Who will be leaving?)

(Improved) By leaving now, you can avoid the heavy traffic.

Dependent clause.   A dependent clause is not capable of standing alone; it depends upon the remainder of the sentence for its meaning. Dependent clauses function as nouns, adjectives, or adverbs. A dependent clause contains a subject and a verb, but it shows its dependence by the linking word which joins it to the main clause.

Direct address.   A direct address construction is one in which a speaker or a writer addresses another person directly.

Edward, please close the door.

Direct object.   The direct object is the person or thing directly affected by the action of the verb.

Mary threw the *softball*. (direct object)

Elliptical clause.   An elliptical clause is a clause from which a word or words have been omitted. The omitted element is understood from other words or from the context. An elliptical clause is usually a dependent clause with its subject and part of its predicate omitted, since these are clearly understood from the main clause. In the following examples, the words shown in brackets are often omitted in speaking and writing.

While [we were] drifting downstream, we noticed a crew of student volunteers removing cans and bottles from the bank.

Although [he is] in Boston frequently, my friend rarely goes to the shopping district.

Essential (or restrictive) clause.   An essential clause is part of the basic meaning of a sentence. Such clauses are not set off with commas.

The car *that you painted* was bought by my brother.

Etymology.   Etymology refers to the history of a word as shown by tracing its phonetic, graphic, and semantic development since its earliest occurrence in the language.

Expletive.   An expletive is a word such as *it* or *there* used merely to get a sentence started.

There were three drivers in our car pool.

Fused sentence.   A fused sentence occurs when two or more main clauses are joined without any punctuation or coordinating conjunction between them.

He could not believe his eyes spare tires and tools were strewn all over the highway.

Gender.   Gender is the characteristic of nouns and pronouns that indicates whether the thing named is masculine (man, boy, he), feminine (woman, girl, she), or neuter (pencil, stone, it).

Gerund.   A gerund is a verb form ending in *ing* which is used as a noun.

Buying is your responsibility.

Gerund phrase.   A gerund phrase is a group of words containing a gerund plus its objects, complements, or modifiers.

Buying new fall dresses is what he does best.

Independent clause (or main clause).   An independent (or main) clause makes a complete statement and may stand alone; that is, it makes reasonable sense if the remainder of the sentence is omitted.

Although I should have been working last night, *I decided to go bowling.*

Indirect object.   The indirect object is the person or thing indirectly affected by the action of the verb. Indirect objects usually tell to whom or for whom something was done or given.

Dad gave *Tony* an electric train.

Infinitive.   An infinitive consists of *to* plus a verb form. Infinitives are used as nouns, adjectives, or adverbs.

To win is her ambition. (noun)

Mary still has three books *to read.* (adjective)

John signed *to play.* (adverb)

Infinitive phrase.   An infinitive phrase consists of an infinitive plus subjects, objects, complements, or modifiers. It is used as a noun, adjective, or adverb.

Billy wanted *to open the box.*

Interjection.   An interjection expresses emotion or surprise. It has no grammatical connection to the other parts of the sentence in which it appears.

Intransitive verb.   An intransitive verb is one that does not need an object to complete its meaning.

The motor *stopped.*

Linking verb. Linking verbs are those verbs that "link" the subject of the sentence with a predicate noun or a predicate adjective. In addition to forms of *be,* they include verbs of the senses like *feel, look, smell, taste,* and *sound* and a limited number of other verbs like *seem, remain, become,* and *appear.*

Mechanics. Mechanics refers to the technical aspects of writing. It includes paragraphing, capitalization, use of italics, use of figures for numbers, abbreviations, and appropriate footnote and bibliography form.

Modifier. Any word or word group functioning as an adjective or an adverb is called a modifier.

Mood. The term *mood* refers to the form of the verb that shows the manner of the action. There are three moods: indicative, imperative, and subjunctive.

The indicative mood states a fact or asks a question.

The door is open.   Is the door open?

The imperative mood expresses a command or makes a request.

Answer the telephone.   Please type this memo as soon as possible.

The subjunctive mood follows clauses of necessity, demand, or wishing and is used in *if, as if,* and *as though* clauses that state conditions which are improbable, doubtful, or contrary to fact.

I *insist* that we *be* heard.   We urge that she *be elected.*

I *wish* I *were* going to the television repair workshop.

If he *were* appointed head of the yard force, I *would* resign immediately.

Nonessential (or nonrestrictive) clause. A nonessential clause is set off with commas because it adds additional information to the main clause but is not necessary to complete the basic meaning of the sentence.

My new tennis racket, *which was endorsed by Chris Evert,* was given to me by my father on my twelfth birthday.

Noun. A noun names a person, place, thing, idea, quality, or activity.

Ms. Jones, city, ball, socialism, honesty, reading

Number. Number is the characteristic of a noun, pronoun, or verb that shows whether one person or thing (singular) or more than one (plural) is indicated.

Noun: boy, boys   Pronoun: she, they   Verb: he works, they play

Paragraph. A paragraph is a group of sentences that develop either a single topic or a small part of a larger topic.

Parallelism. Parallelism is the grammatical principle that words, phrases, or clauses joined in a pair or in a series must be of the same kind. Nouns must be joined with nouns; prepositional phrases must be joined with prepositional phrases; adjective clauses must be joined with adjective clauses. Parallelism breaks down, for example, when a noun is coupled with an adjective or a prepositional phrase is coupled with a participial phrase.

Parenthetical statement. A parenthetical statement is a word, phrase, clause, or sentence, by way of explanation, which is inserted in or added to a statement grammatically complete without it. Parenthetical statements are usually enclosed by parentheses, commas, or dashes.

Participle. A participle is a verb form that functions as an adjective.

falling rain, *broken* dish

Participial phrase. A participial phrase consists of a participle plus an object and modifiers.

Waving the flag briskly, Jim signaled the beginning of the drag race.

Parts of speech. The parts of speech are the eight classes into which words are grouped according to their uses in a sentence: verb, noun, pronoun, adjective, adverb, conjunction, preposition, and interjection.

Person. The term *person* refers to the characteristic of a word that indicates whether a person is speaking (first person), is spoken to (second person), or is spoken about (third person).

Phrase. A phrase is a group of related words not containing both a subject and a predicate. A phrase may be used as the equivalent of a noun, adjective, or adverb.

Predicate. The simple predicate is the verb or verb phrase in a sentence which makes a statement about the action, condition, or state of being of the subject. The complete predicate is the verb plus any complements and modifiers.

Predicate adjective. A predicate adjective follows a linking verb and describes the subject.

Mrs. Johnson is *happy.*

Predicate noun. A predicate noun follows a linking verb and renames the subject or is a word that means the same thing as the subject.

Mac is a good *student.*

Prefix. A prefix is a syllable or word joined to the beginning of another word to alter its meaning or to create a new meaning. Thus, the prefix *pre-* added to *judge* forms *prejudge.*

Preposition. A preposition shows the relation of a noun or pronoun to some other word in the sentence.

A bird flew *over* the house.   The book is *on* the shelf.

A preposition is followed by a noun or pronoun which serves as the object of the preposition. The preposition, its object, and modifiers form a unit called a prepositional phrase.

Mr. Thomas walked *into the old building.*

Principal parts. The principal parts of a verb are the forms from which all other forms are derived: the present, the past, the past participle, and the present participle.

Pronoun. A pronoun is a word that may substitute for a noun.

(noun) Tom is honest.   (pronoun) He is honest.

Punctuation. Punctuation marks are used to indicate relationships between words, phrases, and clauses.

Question. A spoken or written question in its original form is called a direct question.

She then asked, "Who called during my lunch hour?"

An indirect question states the substance of a question without using the speaker's exact words.

She then asked who had called during lunch.

Quotation. A direct quotation contains the exact spoken or written words of others. An indirect quotation includes the substance of a quotation without using the exact words.

Joy said, "I expect to leave after the movie. (direct)

Joy said that she planned to leave after the movie. (indirect)

Recognition span.   Your recognition span is the total number of words your eyes can see at one glance or stop during the act of reading.

Sentence.   A sentence is a group of words that expresses a complete thought and contains a subject and a verb along with any complements and modifiers.

Sentence fragment.   A fragment is a word or group of words not expressing a complete meaning. A sentence fragment is usually a phrase or clause that is incorrectly treated as a sentence.

Squinting modifier.   A "squinting modifier" is an adverb or an adverbial phrase that is placed between two words that it can modify. Because by position it "looks both ways," it results in an ambiguous sentence.

The politician whom we favored enthusiastically praised our energy policy. (Since the adverb *enthusiastically* occupies a position between two verbs that it can modify, *favored* and *praised,* we cannot be sure whether it was the favoring or the praising that was done with enthusiasm. Shifting the adverb to a position before *favored* or after *policy* will relieve the ambiguity.)

Subject.   The subject names the person, place, or thing about which something is said.

Suffix.   A suffix is a syllable or word added to the end of a word to change its meaning, change its grammatical function, or form a new word: *-er* in *stronger, -ness* in *kindness.*

Syllable.   In writing, a syllable refers to a single letter or a group of letters representing one sound.

Tense.   Tense refers to the property of a verb that expresses one of the three divisions of time: present, past, and future.

Topic sentence: A topic sentence is one that expresses the central idea of a paragraph. Most topic sentences are located at the beginning of a paragraph.

Transitional adverb.   Transitional adverbs are words such as *therefore, however, moreover, nevertheless, consequently,* and *hence* that are used to achieve a logical transition between main clauses, whole sentences, and paragraphs.

The weather report sounded ominous; moreover, the announcer urged all vacationers to leave the island as soon as possible.

Transitive verb.   A transitive verb is a verb that requires an object to complete its meaning.

Verb.   A verb expresses action or a state of being.

The ball bounced. (action)

Jim is intelligent. (state of being)

Verb phrase.   A verb phrase consists of a verb plus one, two, or three helping verbs.

is running, has been running, shall have been running

Verbal.   Verbal is the general name applied to participles, gerunds, and infinitives. These words are called "verbals" because they are formed from verbs, but they cannot function as verbs.

Voice.   Voice is the property of a verb that indicates whether the subject acts or is acted upon. A verb is in the active voice when its subject is performing the action.

Carl painted the van.

A verb is in the passive voice when its subject is acted upon.

The van was painted by Carl.

Index

Abbreviations:
  with dates, 211
  of first names, 211
  of Latin expressions, 211
  Ms., Mr., Dr., etc., 210
  of organizations, 211
  of states, months, days of week,
    countries, etc., 210–211
  for states: standard, 53–55
    with zip codes, 53–55
  of streets, avenues, rivers, etc., 211
  of titles or degrees with proper names,
    211
  volume, chapter, and *page,* 211
Absolute construction, defined, 183
Accent marks:
  primary, 10
  secondary, 10
Action verbs, 116, 118
Adjective prepositional phrases,
  167–168
Adjectives:
  defined, 160
  following linking verbs, 163, 165
  irregular, 166
Adverb prepositional phrases, 168
Adverbs:
  defined, 160–161
  following sense verbs, 163
  irregular, 166
  placement of, 18
  use of -ly form, 161–162
Agreement of subject and verb, 155–156
Apostrophe:
  to form plurals of letters, numbers, and
    words referred to as words, 206
  to form possessive adjectives, 206
  to form possessives, 205–206
  to mark omissions, 206
Application form for jobs:
  model of, 69–72
  steps in completing, 68
Appositive expressions:
  defined, 181
  requiring commas, 181
Appositive immediately following a
  pronoun, 138

Bad, badly, 164
Brackets, uses of, 200
Business letters, 52–59
  body of, 57
  complimentary close of, 57–58
  heading of, 52–53
  inside address of, 52–56
  models of, 59
  salutation of, 56–57
  signature of, 58

Capitals:
  after a colon, 214
  for compass directions that name a
    definite section of a country,
    214–215
  for derivatives, 217
  for divisions and books of the Bible,
    217
  for family relationships, 215
  for first letter of sentence, 213
  for geographical locations, 214
  for *O* and *Oh,* 218
  for parts of a hyphenated word,
    217–218
  for proper names, 216
  for religious words referring to a single
    Deity, 217
  for school and college courses, 218
  for streets, buildings, organizations,
    events, holidays, laws,
    documents, exact names of
    government bodies, and legally
    registered corporate names, 215
  The as a part of a newspaper title, 218
  for titles of books, magazines, plays,
    etc., 216–217
  for titles of persons, 216
Choppy sentences caused by lack of
  subordination, 26
Clauses:
  dangling, 20–21
  defined, 13
  dependent, 14–16, 129
  main, 14, 129
  placement of, 18–19

Colon:
    in Biblical references, 194
    before formal statement, 194
    before a list of appositives, 193–194
    before listed items introduced by "the
        following" or "as follows," 193
    between main clauses, 194
    after salutation in a business letter, 194
    in time reference, 194
    between title and subtitle, 194
Comma:
    before an adverb clause at the end of a
        sentence, 176
    basic rules and patterns, 171
    before conjunctions joining main
        clauses, 187–188
    between coordinate adjectives,
        186–187
    to give special emphasis, 177
    after introductory adverb clauses,
        175–176
    after introductory adverbs, 175
    after introductory phrases containing
        verbals, 177
    after introductory prepositional
        phrases, 176–177
    between items in a series, 185–187
    after mild interjections, 175
    pause as guide to use of, 179
    to prevent misreading, 177
    to set off absolute elements, 183
    to set off appositive expressions, 181
    to set off dates and addresses, 183
    to set off nonessential clauses,
        179–181
    to set off nouns of direct address,
        182–183
    to set off parenthetical expressions,
        181–182
    to set off participial phrases, 181
    to set off a short clause that changes a
        statement into a question or an
        exclamatory sentence, 183
    to set off statements of contrast, 182
    special index for, 172–174
    after transitional expressions, 175
Comma splice, 17–18
Comparative degree of adjectives and
        adverbs, 165–166
Comparison degrees, defined, 165–166
Contractions as part of verb phrase, 117
Coordinating conjunctions, parallel
        constructions with, 23

Correlative conjunctions, parallel
        constructions with, 23

Dangling modifier, 20–21
Dash:
    defined, 201
    to mark a sudden break, 202
    to replace omitted letters, 202
    to separate a listing from the remainder
        of a sentence, 202
    to set off appositives, 201–202
    to set off a complete sentence that
        interrupts the normal order of
        another sentence, 202
Dictionary use, 9–11
    etymology, 10
    grammar, 10
    labels, 11
    meaning, 10
    part of speech, 10
    pronunciation, 10
    spelling entry, 10
    synonyms and antonyms, 10
Direct object:
    compound, 127
    definition of, 112, 118, 127
    how to locate, 127
    placed before the verb for special
        effect, 127
Division of words at end of a line, 60
Double comparison, 167

Ellipsis, use of, 195–196
Emphasis:
    by abrupt change in sentence length,
        30
    by arranging ideas in order of climax,
        29–30
    causing artificial style by overuse, 30
    by keeping reader in suspense, 29
    by placing important words in key
        positions, 29
    by repetition, 30
    by unusual word order, 30
    by use of active voice, 30
Exclamation point, use of, 196
Expletive, defined, 126

Fragment, sentence, 15
Fused sentence, 17–18
Future tense, 32

Gerund:
    defined, 130
    use of possessive pronoun before,
        146–147
Gerund phrase, 130–131
Good, 164–165

Hyphen:
    with fractions, 203
    with numbers from twenty-one
        through ninety-nine, 203
    with prefixes and suffixes, 203–204
    to prevent confusion or awkward
        spelling, 204
    between words used as a single
        adjective before a noun, 203

Infinitive:
    defined, 131
    split, 19
Infinitive phrase:
    confused with prepositional phrase,
        132
    defined, 132
Indirect object:
    compound, 128
    defined, 113, 128
    location of, 128
Informal reports:
    defined, 61
    format of, 61–62
Irregular verbs, 119–120
It:
    as expletive, 126
    as pronoun subject, 126
Italics:
    for foreign words and phrases, 221
    for names of ships, trains, and aircraft,
        221
    for titles of books, newspapers, works
        of art, plays, motion pictures, etc.,
        220
    underlining as indication of, 220
    for words, letters, and numbers
        referred to as such, 220

Job hunting:
    application form (*see* Application form
        for jobs)
    blind ads, 67
    bulletin boards, 67

Job hunting (*Cont.*):
    civil service, 65–66
    employment agencies, 64
    location, preferred, 63
    newspaper ads, 66
    people who can help, 64
    state employment service, 65
    trade publications, 67
Job interview:
    approach to, 84
    conclusion and analysis of, 87–88
    main points to cover in, 85
    other considerations in, 86–87
    preparation for, 83–84
    purpose of, 83
    questions to prepare for, 85–86

Lay, lie, 119
Learning, 1–3
    classroom, 3
    defined, 1
Learning environment, 2–3
Lie, lay, 119
Linking verbs, 114, 118
Logical sentences, 30–32

Memorandum:
    defined, 61
    model of, 61
Modifier:
    dangling, 20–21
    defined, 160
    misplaced, 18–19
    placement of, 18–19

Numbers:
    in addresses, 213
    of antecedents of pronouns, 141–142
    beginning sentences with, 212
    in dates, 212
    for divisions and pages of a book, 213
    for percentages and decimals, 213
    of pronouns, 153–154
    of subjects of verbs, 150–154
    for time of day, 213
Noun clause, defined, 129
Nouns:
    collective, number of, 151–152
    defined, 124
    as subjects, 125

Paragraphs:
  checklist for revising, 50
  coherence in, 44–50
    by chronological (time) order,
      44–45
    by concluding with a general
      statement, 45–46
    by order of importance, 45
    by progression from general to the
      particular, 45
    by repetition, 49
    by transitional expressions, 49–50
    by use of pronouns, 49
  defined, 37
  unity in, 44
Parallel constructions, 22–23
  to make comparisons, 23
Parentheses:
  with figures or letters in enumerations,
    200
  position of, with other marks of
    punctuation, 199–200
  with question mark to express
    uncertainty, 200
  to set off additional information, 199
Parenthetical expressions, list of, 182
Participial phrases:
  defined, 181
  requiring commas, 181
Past tense, 32
Perfect tenses, 32
Period:
  after abbreviations, 195
  after courtesy questions, 195
  after each letter and number in an
    outline, 195
  after indirect questions, 195
  after a sentence, 195
Phrases:
  dangling, 20–21
  gerund, 130–131
  infinitive, 132
  introductory, 21
  placement of, 18–19
  verb, 116–117, 125
Plagiarism, 96
Positive degree of adjectives and
  adverbs, 165–166
Predicate:
  compound, 14
  defined, 13
Predicate adjective, 114, 118

Predicate noun:
  defined, 114, 118, 127
  placed before the verb for special
    effect, 127
Prefixes, 7–8
Prepositional phrase:
  confused with infinitive phrase, 132
  defined, 132, 167–168
Prepositions:
  defined, 132
  list of, 168
Present tense, 32
Pronouns:
  agreement with antecedent, 141–142
  defined, 136
  forms of, 136–137
  number of, 153–154
  reference of, 143–144

Question mark, 196
Quotation marks, 196–199
  for dialogue, 197
  for direct quotations, 196–197
  with long indented passages, 197
  position of, with other punctuation
    marks, 198
  with quotation of two or more
    paragraphs, 197
  for quotations within quotations, 197
  for titles, 198
  with words, letters, or figures spoken of
    as such, 198

Raise, rise, 120
Reading, 4–6
  improving reading skills, 5–6
  increasing vocabulary, 7–9
  recognition span, 5
  relationship to writing, 4–5
  stop time, 5–6
Recognition span, 5
Reports, informal, 61–62
Research paper:
  bibliography of, 91–92
    form of entries, 100
    sample entries, 100–102
  checklist for outlines, 93
  footnotes in, 94–96
    form of entries, 97–98
    sample entries, 98–100
  final draft, checklist for, 97
  first draft, 96–97